Relationship Marketing

Relationship Marketing

ROBERT W. PALMATIER

MARKETING SCIENCE INSTITUTE
Cambridge, Massachusetts

Contents

A Theoretical Perspective of Relationship Marketing

An Applied Perspective of Relationship Marketing

Foreword

The 2006-08 MSI research priorities were given the title, "The Connected Customer," to reflect the increasing importance of understanding how customers and the firm interact before making key marketing decisions. Nothing is more fundamental to understanding these interactions than an analysis of the underlying relationships that either have been built or have the potential to be built between customers and firms.

In this monograph, *Relationship Marketing*, the seventh in our Relevant Knowledge Series, Robert Palmatier of the University of Washington brings his outstanding combination of senior executive and academic experience to bear on this critical marketing issue, and takes both a theoretical and applied look at the relationship between buyer and seller.

While much of the attention to relationship marketing has been on financial issues such as measuring lifetime value and managing loyalty programs, Palmatier takes a more strategic perspective by emphasizing the importance of aligning a company's business strategy with its relationship marketing strategy. In addition, he stresses the fact that marketing investments should be focused on what he calls social programs—communications activities between buyer and seller—and structural programs—policies and procedures established between the parties such as electronic ordering and inventory replenishing systems. Palmatier notes that these kinds of programs are more effective in establishing and maintaining long-term customer relationships than financially oriented programs.

Relationship Marketing offers useful perspectives to both academic researchers interested in better understanding the conceptual underpinnings of relationships and managers seeking to build effective relationships with customers. We are very pleased to add it to our Relevant Knowledge Series and we thank Robert Palmatier for his contribution.

Russell S. Winer
New York University
MSI Executive Director 2007-09

Acknowledgments

I would like to acknowledge my coauthors, Todd Arnold, Rajiv P. Dant, Robert F. Dwyer, Kenneth R. Evans, Eric Fang, Srinath Gopalakrishna, Dhruv Grewal, Rajdeep Grewal, Abbie Griffin, Mark B. Houston, Cheryl Burke Jarvis, Frank R. Kardes, Vijaykumar Krishnan, Lisa K. Scheer, and Jan-Benedict E. M. Steenkamp, all of whom have contributed to many of the ideas and findings represented in this work. I also appreciate the support that the Marketing Science Institute (MSI) and the Institute for the Study of Business Markets (ISBM) have given me for many of the primary research projects on which this monograph draws.

Executive Summary

Relationship marketing (RM) and customer relationship management have taken a central position in marketing strategy in the past two decades. A confluence of factors, including the transition to service-based economies; advances in communication, logistics, and computing technologies; increased global competition; and faster product commodization have enhanced the salience of "relationship-based loyalty" to *sellers* compared with other marketing mix factors. Moreover, some of these trends are simultaneously increasing *customers'* desire for the unique characteristics found in relationship-based exchanges (e.g., reduced perceived risk, higher trust, enhanced cooperation, and greater flexibility). Thus, in many situations, both sellers and customers are becoming more interested in conducting business transactions embedded within relationships.

For firms who use—or wish to use—relationship marketing in their business, the primary question is, How can relationship marketing be implemented to improve customer loyalty and seller's sales and profits? Several important managerial takeaways, discussed at length in the monograph, are summarized below.

Minimize Conflict

The factor with the most significant impact on customer relationship quality is unresolved conflict. Existing research clearly demonstrates that conflict between sellers and customers can quickly wreak havoc—destroying trust, commitment, and, ultimately, a relationship built through many years of investment. To avoid and reduce conflict, selling firms must ensure that their business processes are aligned to their relationship marketing strategy. The company culture must emphasize the importance of resolving conflict, and must institute formal systems for correcting customer issues.

The Role of Boundary Spanners

The individual boundary-spanning personnel with whom customers interface often represent the most critical vehicle for building and maintaining strong customer relationships. In many cases, a firm's primary relationship marketing investment should go toward hiring, training, and continually motivating boundary-spanning employees. If possible, firms should align dedicated, competent employees to each customer to take full advantage of the powerful impact of such relationships. At the same time, firms must recognize that loyalty generated from customer–salesperson relationships are often "owned" by the salesperson and can be lost if the salesperson moves to another firm. Thus, firms building relational-based loyalty must balance the benefits from employee-customer relationships with the impact of employee turnover. If facing high turnover, sellers should increase the consistency across boundary spanners, reallocate spending from social to structural programs, and reduce boundary spanners' discretionary control of RM programs to increase seller-owned loyalty and reduce salesperson-owned loyalty.

What Type of RM Program?

Relationship marketing investments should be allocated primarily to social and structural programs rather than financial programs. Social programs appear to generate the highest returns. Relationship marketing programs aimed at increasing communication—the amount, the frequency, and the quality—are especially effective early in the lifecycle, because communication is a strong driver of relationship quality and future relationship growth or relational velocity.

Structural programs, such as electronic order-processing interfaces, customized packaging, and other policy or procedural changes, also enhance relationships between the customer and the selling firm. Structural RM programs should target high-volume, existing, or growing customers, because a larger sales volume supports implementation costs and often provides more value to customers with high-frequency interaction.

In contrast, firms should minimize their proactive use of financial RM programs (e.g., price reductions, rebates, discounts) and instead consider these programs only as price/volume discounts or competitive responses. Most financial programs simply cannot generate positive short-term returns or build long-term relational loyalty. In the worst cases, financial programs can negatively impact customer–seller relationships, depending on the accompanying message on who and why the benefit is being provided.

Understand the Customer

Sellers' relationship marketing returns can be enhanced by better understanding the customer's perspective. In particular, selling firms that can measure and appreciate their customers' relationship orientation—that is, their need and desire for a relationship—can enjoy significant benefits. If a customer has a low need (i.e., low relationship orientation), relationship marketing investments will not only generate poor returns but can actually damage the exchange by increasing customer perceptions of hassles and exchange inefficiencies.

Alternatively, a customer with high relationship orientation—one who both wants and needs a close relationship—represents the very best target for relationship marketing. A number of factors are shown to increase a customer's relationship orientation. Industry relational norms, customer relational-centric reward systems, product dependence and involvement, and any factors increasing a customer's uncertainty or risk will increase a customer's relationship orientation and thus, a seller's relationship marketing effectiveness.

When and How to Implement Programs

To leverage its relationship marketing investments, a seller should time a relationship marketing benefit to when the customer's need is at its peak, and to when that benefit will provide the most value. Moreover, designing programs to increase customers' perceptions of the seller's free will, benevolence, risk, and cost in providing the benefits will influence customer gratitude.

Understanding and managing gratitude and its role in building and maintaining reciprocity norms appears to play an important part in effective relationship marketing. Grateful customers are psychologically "hardwired" to feel the need to reciprocate. Sellers should give customers an opportunity to reciprocate soon after receiving a RM benefit, which takes advantage of high levels of gratitude, prevents guilt rationalization, and leads to the formation of reciprocity norms. Ensuring that programs have some random or discretionary element is important, otherwise the program becomes integrated into the overall value proposition of the offering, which only generates one-to-one payoffs (i.e., a quid pro quo mentality).

Keep Growing

Common wisdom suggests that long-term customers have the strongest and highest-paying relationships, but research demonstrates that this is not always the case. Instead, the highest-performing relationships are the ones that are still growing. Once a relationship peaks and enters a maintenance phase its effect on performance diminishes. If the customer no longer requires a relationship, the seller should either move that customer to a more transactional, low-cost interface or reinvigorate the exchange with new offerings, new personnel, or other changes. Continuing to invest RM efforts in customers that no longer value the relationship is inefficient and may even be detrimental to the exchange.

Ongoing Assessment

To understand the effectiveness of RM efforts, firms should measure their relational assets on an ongoing basis. Such measures should recognize the multidimensional aspects of customer relationships (e.g., quality, breadth, composition, growth/velocity), and metrics should provide feedback to individual boundary spanners or teams (e.g., input to compensation and bonuses). For interfirm relationships, sellers should capture both the breadth (number of contacts) and composition (authority and diversity) of their customer contact portfolio and focus their efforts on any identified weaknesses. It may seem obvious to state that investments require consistent measurement to determine their returns, but such actions remain relatively rare in relationship marketing practice. These ongoing assessments should not concentrate solely on customer perspectives, but also on the overall selling organization. For example, selling firms should conduct internal audits that ensure various organizational elements—such as strategy, leadership, culture, structures, and control—continually and consistently align with the firms' relationship marketing objectives. Firms must recognize that building and maintaining strong customer relationships are dependent on both dedicated RM programs as well as diverse elements of the overall organization.

Introduction

The importance of relationships in business exchanges can be traced to Homeric Greece, and the critical impact of idiosyncratic, interpersonal relationships has been well documented throughout history. Yet relationship marketing and customer relationship management have emerged as specific priorities for marketing academics and managers only in the past few decades. The relatively recent explosion of research papers, popular business books, and customer relationship management initiatives in Western cultures stems from a confluence of factors, including the transition to service-based economies; advances in communication, logistics, and computing technologies; increased global competition; and faster product commodization. These trends have enhanced the salience of "relationship-based loyalty" to *sellers* compared with other marketing-mix factors and increased desire on the part of *customers* for many unique characteristics found in "relationship-based exchanges" (e.g., reduced perceived risk, higher trust, enhanced cooperation, greater flexibility). Thus, in many situations, both sellers and customers are becoming more interested in conducting business transactions embedded within relationships.

This monograph synthesizes prior research to give academics and managers a snapshot of what we know and don't know about relationship marketing. I discuss eight general issues regarding relationship marketing, divided into two sections with varying degrees of relevance to scholars and managers. The first section provides theoretical insights by focusing on three questions: (1) What is relationship marketing? (2) How does relationship marketing work? and (3) How do relationships change over time? These topics may be especially interesting to academics and managers who want a foundational understanding of relationship marketing.

The second section summarizes key empirical findings critical to the application of relationship marketing. More specifically, by integrating and extending past research, the text offers insight into four important managerial issues: (1) understanding relationship marketing's financial impact, (2) building and maintaining strong relationships, (3) targeting and adapting relationship marketing strategies, and (4) enhancing performance through best practices. This section should be especially interesting to practitioners of relationship marketing.

The final chapter outlines research directions and topics that may advance relationship marketing research and practice in the future.

Robert W. Palmatier

A Theoretical Perspective of Relationship Marketing

1

What Is Relationship Marketing?

To inform this crucial and foundational question—what is relationship marketing?—this text evaluates three viewpoints. First, it presents the scope and definition of relationship marketing. Second, it compares relationship marketing with related marketing areas to evaluate its potential overlap with other domains in marketing. Third, it places relationship marketing within a historical context by describing its evolution over time.

Definition

The American Marketing Association's definition of marketing, revised in 2004, indicates that "marketing is an organizational function and a set of processes for creating, communicating, and delivering value to customers and for *managing customer relationships* in ways that benefit the organization and its stakeholders" (emphasis added). Thus, the overall definition of marketing identifies the process of managing relationships as one of its key charters, parallel to more traditional marketing-mix factors. The domain that deals with "relationships," termed relationship marketing and often attributed to Berry (1983), has been defined in many different ways by scholars from various research perspectives (Harker 1999).

An analysis of some of the most prevalent definitions suggests that three key aspects constitute relationship marketing (e.g., Grönroos 1997; Sheth and Parvatiyar 2000), as Table 1, p. 6, which provides a summary of common relationship marketing definitions, makes clear. The first aspect deals with engagement activities across stages of the relationship lifecycle and thereby implicitly recognizes that relationships are dynamic processes that develop over time through typical stages, such that relationship marketing activities and exchange characteristics systematically vary across those stages (Dwyer and Oh 1987; Wilson 1995). The number of stages and terminology used differ slightly among researchers, but the vast majority of definitions imply four general stages: identifying, developing, maintaining, and terminating.

The second key aspect deals with the target or scope of relationship marketing activities; whereas some definitions are restricted to customer relationships, others include relationships with any constituent (e.g., internal departments, competitors, customers, suppliers). Relationship marketing tactics vary across these different types of "partners," but there is little reason to expect that the underlying theories, frameworks, or models change fundamentally (Morgan and Hunt 1994). Thus, opening the scope of relationship marketing practice to any target "entity" seems appropriate. Furthermore, recent research reemphasizes the importance of building relationships with parties other than customers by arguing that firms often compete through their network of interfirm relationships (Rindfleisch and Moorman 2003; Sivadas and Dwyer 2000).

Another facet of this relationship target pertains to the unit of analysis or level of the relationship. Relationships can be evaluated between individuals (person-to-person, interpersonal), between an individual and a firm or group of people (person-to-firm, firm-to-person), and between firms (firm-to-firm, interfirm). A large body of empirical evidence demonstrates that relationships form at each of these levels (Doney and Cannon 1997; Palmatier et al. 2007c). In many cases, relationships with multiple targets occur simultaneously and have divergent effects on performance (Palmatier, Scheer, and Steenkamp 2007).

The third and final aspect deals with the locus of benefits derived from relationship marketing activities. In other words, does the success of relationship marketing efforts depend only on the perspective of the implementer (e.g., seller), or must both parties' outcomes be evaluated? In practice, relationship marketing needs to generate benefits for both parties, even if one party's benefit is limited to social rewards, to achieve the implementers' long-term performance objectives. But by recognizing that relationship marketing is not altruistically motivated but rather initiated by a party to achieve specific goals, a unidirectional perspective appears most relevant, even though the most effective relationship marketing programs generate value for both parties. Such a unidirectional perspective is driven more by the need to remain consistent with relationship marketers' motivations and evaluation perspectives than by the belief that only one party gains value from developing strong and enduring relational bonds. For example, firms that initiate relationship marketing judge program effectiveness from the returns on their investments (ROI); considerations of the value generated *for the customer* from these efforts rarely represent an end in themselves but rather provide a means to increase program effectiveness.

Some language used to describe relationship marketing seems altruistic or unrealistically benevolent, or as described by Egan (2004, p. 23), "Altruistic sentiments implemented by [relationship marketing] might seem to contradict the fact that the profit motive [is] still a principal business driver." Underlying such "win–win" terminology is usually the recognition that firms and managers are driven by profit motives, so unprofitable relationships should be terminated and relationship-building investments should target optimal returns. Thus, though relationship marketing entails cooperation and co-value creation with a long-term perspective—rather than a short-term, transaction, manipulation, or competitive focus—it is initiated for the ultimate long-term gain of the implementer. When researchers include the termination of relationships as an aspect of relationship marketing, they implicitly acknowledge their unilateral perspective. For example, most researchers and managers recommend that sellers terminate or adapt unprofitable customer relationships, even if the customer is gaining value from them.

Integrating these three aspects results in the following definition: *Relationship marketing (RM) is the process of identifying, developing, maintaining, and terminating relational exchanges with the purpose of enhancing performance.*

Overlap with Other Marketing Domains

Various other domains or areas in marketing overlap with relationship marketing, and in these fields, academics have studied similar antecedents and outcomes. Relationship marketing shares many commonalities with services marketing, business-to-business marketing, channels marketing, brand management, and customer relationship management. However, distinctions exist. For example, RM's overlap with service, business-to-business, and channel marketing may be clarified by differentiating their focus on improving performance in contexts with specific features (e.g., intangible services, exchanges between firms or channel members) versus RM's concentration on improving performance by changing relationships. Relationship marketing also applies to many different contexts with varying degrees of effectiveness. For example, a meta-analysis of more than 38,000 relationships shows that building strong relationships is more effective for improving performance among services than among product offerings, in business-to-business versus business-to-consumer markets, and for channel partners rather than direct customers (Palmatier et al. 2006). Thus, not surprisingly, research and practice in services, business-to-business, and channels contexts often include relational constructs. Early

Table 1
Summary and Analysis of Relationship Marketing Definitions

Definition	Stage	
	Identifying	Developing
"Attracting, maintaining, and—in multi-service organizations— enhancing customer relationships." Berry (1983, p. 25)		x
"[P]rocess of identifying and establishing, maintaining, enhancing, and when necessary terminating relationships with customers and other stakeholders, at a profit, so that the objectives of all parties involved are met, where this is done by a mutual giving and fulfillment of promises." Grönroos (1997, p. 407)	x	x
Based on synthesis of 26 definitions of relationship marketing: "organization engaged in proactively creating, developing and maintaining committed, interactive and profitable exchanges with selected customers [partners] over time." Harker (1999, p. 16)	x	x
"Relationship marketing refers to all marketing activities directed toward establishing, developing, and maintaining successful relational exchanges." Morgan and Hunt (1994, p. 22)	x	x
"Relationship marketing is the ongoing process of engaging in cooperative and collaborative activities and programs with immediate and end-user customers to create or enhance mutual economic value at reduced cost." Sheth and Parvatiyar (2000, p. 9)	x	x
Definition based on analysis of extant relationship marketing definitions: Relationship marketing is the process of identifying, developing, maintaining, and terminating relational exchanges with the purpose of enhancing performance.	x	x

Maintaining	Terminating	Target/Scope		Locus of Benefits	
		Customer only	All	Implementer	Bilateral
X		X			
X	X		X	X	X
X		X		X	
X			X		X
X		X			X
X	X		X	X	

research in the service context also provides the roots for many key RM concepts (Berry 1983, 1995).

In reality, relationship marketing and branding strategies that focus on building brand equity also overlap. Researchers suggest that relationships and brands represent two critical sources of intangible, market-based assets that can be leveraged into superior financial performance (Srivastava, Shervani, and Fahey 1998). But brand equity represents the differential effect of brand knowledge on customer action, such that customers behave more favorably toward a product when they can identify the brand (Keller 1993). Others argue that brand equity may be "a fundamentally product-centered concept" that does not capture drivers of customer behavior fully (Rust, Lemon, and Zeithaml 2004, p. 110). Although RM and branding activities similarly focus on building intangible customer assets that positively influence customer loyalty, purchase behaviors, or financial performance while reducing marketing costs, they differ fundamentally in that branding focuses on "product(s)" with extensions to the firm, whereas RM primarily focuses on "relationship(s)" and their extensions to the firm. The distinction between branding and RM remains clear at the core level of products versus relationships, but as customers develop attitudes toward and beliefs about the overall firm, the individual impact of brands and relationships becomes difficult to separate. Thus, overall customer equity is generated from both brand equity and relational equity. The relative importance of brands compared with relationships often depends on the context and/or the researcher's perspective. For example, when a survey asks a customer to report on his or her "trust in a firm," the question comprises both product- and relationship-based trust. Differentiating brands and relationships pragmatically requires identifying the constructs measured and the focal referent of the construct; that is, relationship marketing focuses on the relationship (versus product) and measures relational characteristics such as trust, commitment, reciprocity norms, cooperation, and conflict.

The distinction between branding and RM remains clear at the core level of products versus relationships, but the effect of brands and relationships on a customer's attitude toward the firm is difficult to separate.

The overlap between relationship marketing and customer relationship management may be simply a semantic issue because the terms are sometimes used interchangeably. A recent definition of customer relationship management from the *Journal of Marketing*, based on a synthesis of the literature, suggests that customer relationship management is a subcomponent of RM with the following additional caveats (Payne and Frow 2005, p. 168):

1. Restricts the relationship target to "key customers and customer segments."

2. "[U]nites the potential of relationship marketing and IT [information-technology]."

3. Focuses more on the tactical through an "integration of process, people, operations, and marketing capabilities that is enabled through information, technology, and applications."

Thus, *customer relationship management (CRM) is the managerially relevant application of relationship marketing across an organization focused on customers, which leverages IT to achieve performance objectives.* If RM is the science or physics of relationships, then CRM represents its application or engineering. Because extant research often fails to differentiate between RM and CRM, this monograph uses the term relationship marketing in its broad form, with the recognition that it often encompasses aspects of customer relationship management as well.

If relationship marketing is the science or physics of relationships, then customer relationship management represents its application or engineering.

Historical Perspective

The emergence of RM as a separate academic domain of marketing in the 1980s and 1990s becomes more comprehensible from a historical perspective. Researchers argue that RM represents a "paradigm shift in marketing" from its previous focus on "transactions," in which firms use the "4P model" to manage marketing-mix variables (Grönroos 1994, p. 4; Sheth and Parvatiyar 2000). But is RM really a new phenomenon? What underlying trends or factors drive such a change? To answer these questions, this text offers a historical perspective of relationship marketing thought and practice.

Researchers have made the compelling case that relational-based exchange was the norm for most of recorded history; the anomaly of transaction-based marketing emerged only in the early 1900s. Thus, relationship marketing "is really a rebirth of marketing practices of the pre-industrial age" (Sheth and Parvatiyar 1995, p. 399). Prior to the industrial age, most exchange occurred in local markets, where farmers and craftspeople (producers) sold their products directly to end users. Producers represented both manufacturers and retailers, and embedded relationships between producers and consumers provided the trust and business norms necessary to conduct the transaction because few institutionalized protections existed. Similarly, relationships led to confidence among traders in the transactions of goods not locally produced. Sheth and Parvatiyar (1995) offer numerous examples of trade, which would only occur among groups with ongoing relationships—such as among traders along the historical "silk route"—that built trust over time and examples of the use of family names in specific industries that branded relational trust. Thus, though the terminology and specific academic focus on RM are relatively new, the underlying importance of relationships for understanding exchange performance absolutely is not.

Relational-based exchange was the norm for most of recorded history; the anomaly of transaction-based marketing emerged only in the early 1900s.

Mass production and consumption during the industrial revolution changed the dynamics between producers and consumers. Producers took advantage of the economies of scale associated with mass production to produce a large volume of goods at low cost, but these voluminous goods also required transportation, storage, and sales across a larger geographic area and customer base to dispose of them. Many consumers relocated to manufacturing centers and cities, away from agricultural areas, which required the transportation and storage of goods to support these new population centers. Moreover, mass production generated the need for aggressive sales and promotions to create sufficient demand for the increased volume of goods. In aggregate, industrialization led to new industries, or "middlemen," focused on transportation, storage, selling, and retailing (Bartels 1962). As these new channels competed for business, often with similar or indistinguishable products, exchanges became more transactional and pricing grew to represent a more, if not the most, salient component of the offering. Institutional and functional economists operating against this backdrop investigated the functions performed by wholesalers and retailers in an exchange to develop early marketing thought (Alderson 1965).

This functional economic view of marketing evolved over time by integrating psychological and sociological viewpoints, but product-centric transactions remained the dominant paradigm: marketers varied marketing-mix factors (i.e., price, product, place, and promotion) to achieve business objectives

(Grönroos 1994; Sheth and Parvatiyar 1995; Vargo and Lusch 2004). This state of affairs brings us to our second question: what underlying trends or factors are shifting marketing back to a relationship focus? The answer probably lies not in any one trend but rather in a convergence of many factors.

For example, consider the shift to service economies in many developed countries; services now represent approximately 85% of the U.S. economy. Services typically are produced and delivered by the same organization, which means removing the "middleman" and reinforcing the bonds between producer and consumer. In addition, services compared with products are more intangible, less consistent, more perishable, and harder to evaluate, which generally makes customers and the sellers' boundary-spanning personnel more involved in production and consumption, sometimes even requiring co-production (Zeithaml, Parasuraman, and Berry 1985). Closer interactions between customers and sellers make customer–seller relationships more critical for services than for products, and the intangibility of the offering makes the benefits of trust more important (Palmatier et al. 2006). As economies transition from product- to service-based, customer–seller relationships develop (i.e., fewer middlemen, higher interaction levels) and become more important to customers (i.e., reducing risk and increasing need for cooperation).

Another key trend promoting the use of RM relates to advances in technology. Communication and logistics improvements support direct transactions between producers and consumers at great distances by, in effect, duplicating preindustrial local bazaars on a global or at least national level. Consumers desire the trust and confidence of a relational-based exchange to transact in this global bazaar (Sheth and Parvatiyar 1995). In addition, advances in IT and communications provide sellers with the tools to target, implement, and evaluate their specific RM programs rather than rely solely on a mass marketing approach.

Also driving firms to concentrate on customer retention and loyalty programs are increases in global competition and customer churn rates, especially for commodity products and service, in markets in which prices from many manufacturers in many countries are transparent to consumers Sellers require non–price-based strategies to increase customer loyalty and thus potentially support premium prices or at least minimize price erosion. Moreover, analyses that identify higher costs associated with acquiring versus retaining customers reinforce loyalty-building strategies, and RM programs have become primary tools to support such goals.

Even in business-to-business markets, initiatives such as Total Quality Management (TQM) and the need to develop close relationships with suppliers to support rapid product development have increased firms' desire to build long-lasting bonds with their suppliers and other business partners (Sheth and Parvatiyar 1995).

2

How Does Relationship Marketing Work?

Because researchers from many different disciplines have studied the impact of relationships on human behavior, marketing has a rich theoretical landscape from which to draw to understand relationship marketing. Many of these different disciplines take central positions in the development of RM theory. This monograph organizes that resulting theory into four parts. The first part details each discipline's contribution to RM theory as it has evolved over time. Table 2 summarizes the evolution of marketing theory and outlines the contributions of different theoretical perspectives and disciplines. The second and third parts present two integrative models of RM which result from syntheses of multiple theoretical perspectives, one focused on interfirm (business-to-business [B2B]) and the other on interpersonal (B2B and business-to-consumer [B2C]) relationship marketing. Finally, the last section discusses the impact of multilevel relationships, which develop and operate simultaneously within an exchange (e.g., customer–salesperson, customer–selling firm).

Evolution of Relationship Marketing Theory

The roots of marketing and relationship marketing theory stem from economics. When Wroe Alderson (1958, pp. 27, 28) extended the institutional economics view that exchanges are driven by value maximization and market efficiency, he argued that because people are involved, marketing thought must include the sociological factors of "power structure" and "two-way exchange of commitments," as well as the social psychological factors of "communication" and "emotional reactions."

Bagozzi (1975, p. 32) further refined marketing's focus by applying "exchange theory" to what he considers the two key questions of marketing theory: "(1) Why do people and organizations engage in exchange relationships? and (2) How are exchanges created, resolved, or avoided?" Consistent with the emergence of middlemen in business exchanges, channel researchers employed

Table 2

Evolution of Relationship Marketing Theory

Period	Theory and/or Source Discipline	Key Contribution
1950s and 1960s	Institutional economics, sociology, and psychology	Integrated sociological and psychological factors into prevalent institutional economic perspective of rational economic actors.
1970s	Exchange theory (sociology)	Redirected marketing thought by applying "exchange theory" to two key questions in marketing theory: (1) Why do people and organizations engage in exchange relationships? and (2) How are exchanges created, resolved, or avoided?
1970s and 1980s	Power and dependence theory (sociology)	Consistent with the criticality of "middlemen" to business during this period, offered power/dependence among channel partners as the critical factor in understanding exchange relationship and performance.
1980s and 1990s	Relational contracting theory (political science) and social exchange theory (sociology)	Integrated relational contracting theory with social exchange theory in a dynamic relationship framework. Proposed that relational norms have important roles in guiding relationship behavior in business exchanges.
1990s	Transaction cost economics (economics)	Demonstrated that relationship governance can serve many of the same functions as vertical integration from a transaction cost perspective by suppressing opportunistic behaviors, reducing transaction costs (e.g., safeguarding and monitoring costs), and promoting performance-enhancing investments.

Period	Theory and/or Source Discipline	Key Contribution
1990 to 2000	Commitment-trust theory of relationship marketing (sociology and psychology)	Extended relationship marketing beyond customer–seller interactions to offer a well-argued theory of relationship marketing that revolves around trust and commitment. This framework provided the default theoretical basis for the majority of relationship marketing research for the next decade.

Emerging Relationship Marketing Theory

Period	Theory and/or Source Discipline	Key Contribution
2000s	Resource-based view of interfirm relationships (management)	Integrated multiple theoretical perspectives within a resource-based view of interfirm exchange by demonstrating that relationship marketing's impact on performance is affected by relational bonds (e.g., trust, commitment), as well as investments (e.g., training, communication) that enhance the efficacy or effectiveness of the relational asset.
2000s	Interfirm relationship marketing based on social exchange and network theories (sociology)	Integrated social network theory to develop an interfirm-specific relationship marketing framework, which shows that in addition to relationship quality (trust, commitment), two other relational drivers are key to understanding the impact of interfirm relationships on performance: relationship breadth and composition.
2000s	Micro-theory of interpersonal relationships (evolutionary psychology and sociology)	Integrated gratitude, guilt, and norms of reciprocity into a dynamic model of intrapersonal relationship marketing based on a evolutionary or quasi-Darwinian perspective of relationships and cooperative behavior.

the power-dependence framework from social exchange theory, developed in sociology, to understand relationships between channel partners (Emerson 1962). Specifically, early channel researchers proposed a positive effect of dependence on performance because the dependent partner wanted to maintain the relationship to achieve its goals rather than undertake the difficulty or cost of finding a replacement partner (El-Ansary 1975; Frazier 1983). Empirical research generally supports the positive role of interdependence among exchange partners, in that it enhances cooperation and performance, whereas asymmetric dependence (dependence imbalance) can generate conflict and undermine cooperation (Bucklin and Sengupta 1993; Gassenheimer, Davis, and Dahlstrom 1998; Hibbard, Kumar, and Stern 2001; Kumar, Scheer, and Steenkamp 1995a).

Recent research recasts dependence as a contextual or background variable rather than a prime driver of relationship performance (Morgan and Hunt 1994; Palmatier, Dant, and Grewal 2007). This perspective indicates that the dependence between relationship partners is important because it affects the development and maintenance of a relationship, not because it is an immediate "precursor" of relationship performance (Palmatier, Dant, and Grewal 2007, p. 183). Thus, though early relational exchange research gave dependence a central theoretical role, it has since been recast in a supporting role.

Dwyer, Schurr, and Oh's (1987) classic paper integrated relational contract theory (Macaulay 1963; Macneil 1980) with social exchange theory (Blau 1964; Thibaut and Kelley 1959) to develop a framework of buyer–seller relationships in which exchanges lie on a continuum from discrete to relational transactions. Dwyer and colleagues also offer a wide range of relational constructs (trust, commitment, norms, dependence, justice, conflict, cooperation, and communication) that they suggest are instrumental in relationship development and dissolution. Perhaps due to their significant influence, the next 20 years of RM research, grounded in social exchange and relational contracting theory, focused on proposing and empirically testing nomological frameworks based on the relational constructs outlined in Dwyer, Schurr, and Oh's (1987) conceptual paper.

Relational exchange theory, which builds on relational contracting theory, argues that relational norms, whether alone or in conjunction with commitment and trust, enable relationship partners to respond more effectively to changing conditions and project their actions and responses into the future by preventing self-interest-seeking behaviors, which in turn improves exchange performance (Kaufmann and Dant 1992; Macneil 1980). Relational norms positively influence cooperative behaviors and financial performance (Cannon,

Achrol, and Gundlach 2000; Siguaw, Simpson, and Baker 1998) and suppress conflict (Jap and Ganesan 2000).

Another empirically well-supported theoretical framework used to understand the effectiveness of relational governance among firms is transaction cost economics (Rindfleisch and Heide 1997; Williamson 1985, 1975), which assumes that because people use guile to serve their self-interests, relational-specific investments in an exchange must be monitored and safeguarded from opportunistic behaviors by partners (Rindfleisch and Heide 1997). As the level of relational-specific investments increases, people either vertically integrate to avoid monitoring and safeguarding costs or develop relational governance structures (i.e., build relationships) to safeguard these investments and minimize the need to monitor. Empirical research in marketing supports the premise that relationships among partners support performance-enhancing, relational-specific investments while reducing transaction costs and opportunistic behaviors (Gassenheimer, Davis, and Dahlstrom 1998; Heide and John 1990; John 1984; Wathne and Heide 2000; Weiss and Anderson 1992).

Morgan and Hunt (1994, p. 22), in "The Commitment-Trust Theory of Relationship Marketing" (perhaps the most influential RM paper to date), posit that "presence of relationship commitment and trust is central to successful relationship marketing, not power." On the basis of research grounded in social exchange theory, marriage, and organizational behavior, they argue that relationship commitment, "an enduring desire to maintain a valued relationship" (Moorman, Zaltman, and Deshpandé 1992, p. 316), and trust, the "confidence in an exchange partner's reliability and integrity" (Morgan and Hunt 1994, p. 23), represent the key elements that explain a relationship's impact on performance. Thus, relationship partners who are committed expend extra effort and work to maintain and strengthen relational bonds, which positively influences cooperation, financial performance, and other positive outcomes (Kumar, Hibbard, and Stern 1994; Morgan and Hunt 1994). In addition, trust has a direct effect on relationship outcomes and an indirect effect through its influence on commitment (Ambler, Styles, and Xiucum 1999; Crosby, Evans, and Cowles 1990; Hibbard et al. 2001; Mohr and Spekman 1994). Overall, Morgan and Hunt's (1994) model of RM reduces the scope from Dwyer, Schurr, and Oh's (1987) framework in two key ways: it narrows the relational constructs of interest to trust and commitment and ignores any dynamic relationship effects.

The empirically well-supported commitment–trust theory has provided the default theoretical basis for most relationship research during the past decade (Morgan and Hunt 1994; Palmatier et al. 2006). However, theoretical gaps emerged in the framework during the course of empirical testing through a meta-analysis of more than 111 independent samples covering 38,000 interpersonal and interorganizational relationships (Palmatier et al. 2006). Although this recent research synthesis provides strong empirical support for the critical role of commitment and trust, it also uncovers two major weaknesses. First, relationship investments have a positive direct effect on objective performance, above and beyond the indirect effect mediated by trust and commitment, across both interpersonal and interfirm relationships. This finding suggests that any model must include other performance-enhancing mediators if it wants to capture the positive financial effect of RM fully.

Second, contrary to conventional wisdom, relationship quality, a composite construct that captures multiple aspects or dimensions of a relationship (e.g., trust, commitment, relationship satisfaction), has a stronger impact on objective performance than any single dimension. Thus, Palmatier and colleagues (2006, p. 149) suggest that "[d]ifferent dimensions of a relationship may be synergistic, and superior performance may be possible only when the relationship is sufficiently strong on all critical aspects."

Different aspects or dimensions of a relationship may be synergistic, and performance is optimized only when the relationship is sufficiently strong on all critical aspects.

To integrate these various theoretical perspectives within a single model, recent research uses the results of a longitudinal comparison of the four most common theoretical frameworks; as Palmatier, Dant, and Grewal (2007) show, the dependence structure among interfirm partners is not an immediate precursor of relationship performance but rather provides a contextual backdrop against which relationships may develop, whereas trust, commitment, and relationship investments directly enhance interfirm relationships and financial performance. Thus, similar to the findings of the meta-analysis of relational mediators, this study shows that trust and commitment do not fully mediate the impact of relationship investments on performance outcomes, which again suggests the need to add mediating mechanisms to the theory of RM to capture the full range of performance-enhancing effects.

In addition, the importance of both relational governance constructs (i.e., trust and commitment) and relationship-specific investments to relationship performance are consistent with a resource-based view of interfirm relationships (Dyer and Singh 1998; Jap 1999; Palmatier, Dant, and Grewal 2007). The resource-based view has evolved in management literature to show that resources or assets that are valuable, rare, and difficult to duplicate increase sustainable competitive advantage and lead to superior firm performance (Wernerfelt 1984). Therefore, though trust and commitment increase the quality of the relational bonds necessary for high-performance exchanges, relationship investments improve other performance-enhancing aspects of the exchange. For example, RM can increase joint knowledge about relationship partners and informal communication between partners, which may improve the effectiveness and efficiency of the relational exchange while also increasing trust and commitment.

Furthermore, most prior RM research pertains to interfirm relationships, but the models often are extended to an interpersonal context, even though researchers note the many differences across these two contexts (Iacobucci and Ostrom 1996; Reynolds and Beatty 1999). Some recent RM research has begun to distinguish between relationships between two firms (interfirm) and those between two individuals (interpersonal) to address these differences (Palmatier et al. 2007c; Palmatier, Scheer, and Steenkamp 2007). Specifically, different types of RM activities are more effective at building interpersonal rather than interfirm relationships; in addition, all else being equal, interpersonal relationships have a stronger effect on customer behaviors and financial performance than do interfirm relationships. These results demonstrate the need to distinguish theoretically between interpersonal and interfirm relationships.

Interpersonal relationships have a stronger effect on customer behavior and financial performance than do interfirm relationships.

Researchers have also applied an evolutionary psychology or a "quasi-Darwinian" perspective to marketing relationships (Eyuboglu and Buja 2007; Palmatier et al. 2007b). For example, Eyuboglu and Buja (2007, p. 48) argue that "relationships that survive have passed a process of 'selection.' They are adaptive in the Darwinian sense." Thus, they recast causal arguments about relational constructs as a process in which "selection creates associations," so that factors such as unilateralism, bilateralism, dependence, and environmental adversity affect the survival of marketing relationships. Others apply an evolutionary perspective to specific emotional processes (e.g., gift-gratitude, anger-punishment, guilt-reciprocation) to explain consumer behavior in response to marketers' actions and the underlying effectiveness of RM (Cialdini and Rhoads 2001; Dahl, Honea, and Manchanda 2003; Dahl, Honea, and Manchanda 2005;

Morales 2005; Palmatier et al. 2007b). Although evolutionary psychology provides compelling functional explanations for many observed behaviors that may appear illogical at first glance, these explanations often are criticized as no more than "post hoc stories."

In summary, researchers from many different theoretical perspectives and disciplines have provided insight into how and why RM works and suggested various focal constructs as critical for understanding relationship performance. But theoretical gaps and opportunities for improving our theoretical understanding of why RM works still remain. Five of the most critical are as follows:

1. Identify the missing "relational mechanisms" to explain the significant direct effects of RM activities on objective performance that are not captured by trust and commitment (e.g., relationship efficiency and effectiveness mechanisms).

2. Develop a more dynamic theory of RM that explicitly recognizes the lifecycle and time-varying nature of relationships (e.g., how does Morgan and Hunt's [1994] model of RM differ across relationship lifecycle stages?).

3. Adapt existing RM theory to account for differences in interfirm and interpersonal relationships (e.g., group dynamic and network effects between and within firms).

4. Integrate and synthesize the many extant theories of RM, as well as some new theoretical frameworks, such as the resource-based view, social network theory, and evolutionary psychology, to generate more holistic models of RM (i.e., use a multidisciplinary approach to understand RM).

5. Account for how multilevel relationships (e.g., customer-to-salesperson, customer-to-selling firm) work together to drive exchange performance.

The subsequent parts of this chapter therefore attempt to address these gaps by integrating both past and recent research, proposing theoretically different models of RM for interfirm and interpersonal relationships, providing insight into multilevel relationships, and investigating how relationships develop over time. In addition, these new models integrate research based on new theoretical perspectives, including network theory and evolutionary psychology.

Interfirm Relationship Marketing Theory[1]

A theory of interfirm RM should acknowledge that relationships typically entail groups of employees on both sides of the exchange dyad. Thus, firm-to-firm relationships involve multiple interactions among many people or, in effect, a

Figure 1
Five Drivers of Interfirm Relationship Performance

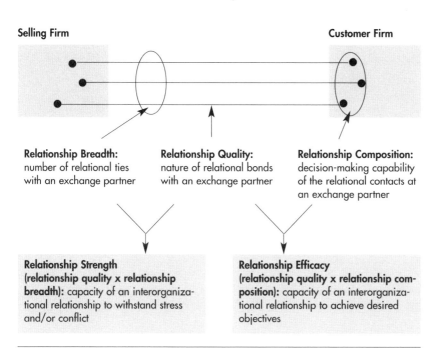

Selling Firm   Customer Firm

Relationship Breadth: number of relational ties with an exchange partner

Relationship Quality: nature of relational bonds with an exchange partner

Relationship Composition: decision-making capability of the relational contacts at an exchange partner

Relationship Strength (relationship quality x relationship breadth): capacity of an interorganizational relationship to withstand stress and/or conflict

Relationship Efficacy (relationship quality x relationship composition): capacity of an interorganizational relationship to achieve desired objectives

Source: Palmatier 2008

network of relationships. Network theory developed in sociology provides valuable insights into the impact of the structural characteristics of interaction among multiple entities (e.g., individuals, firms) within an overall network (Borgatti and Foster 2003; Houston et al. 2004; Van den Bulte and Wuyts 2007), and this network perspective recently has been applied to interfirm relationships to show that not only relationship quality (e.g., trust, commitment) but also relationship breadth (network density) and relationship composition (network diversity/attractiveness) notably influence exchange performance (Palmatier 2008, 2007). A seller's RM activities influence three fundamental drivers of RM effectiveness—relationship quality, breadth, and composition—each of which captures a different and important aspect of interfirm relationships and has a positive impact on the seller's performance outcomes. Moreover, these fundamental drivers appear to work synergistically to enhance relational outcomes. Figure 1 shows a model for understanding the five drivers of interfirm relationship performance. The following discussion demonstrates how each driver influences interfirm relationship performance.

Relationship Quality The caliber of relational bonds with an exchange partner represents *relationship quality*, which parallels the concept of tie strength in network theory (relational bonds between actors) and captures the concepts of relational embeddedness, closeness, and degree of reciprocity in social bond theory (e.g., Rindfleisch and Moorman 2001). According to prior research (Crosby, Evans, and Cowles 1990; Kumar, Scheer, and Steenkamp 1995b), the composite relationship quality construct captures the diverse interaction characteristics required to create a high-caliber relational bond, such as commitment, trust, reciprocity norms, and exchange efficiency. Thus, each construct is related but captures unique aspects of relational bonds; these aspects in turn positively influence specific exchange outcomes. In aggregate, however, they reflect the overall quality ŏr caliber of the bond.

Specifically, commitment represents exchange partners' desire to maintain valued relationships and thus their relational motivation toward partners. As an evaluation of a partner's reliability and integrity, trust generates confidence in the partner's future actions and supports cooperation. Reciprocity norms, the internalized beliefs and expectations a firm holds about the balance of obligations in an exchange, have pervasive impacts on exchange behaviors, though they also take longer to develop. Finally, exchange efficiency—the assessment of time, effort, and resources needed to maintain a relationship—enhances exchange performance because "governance structures that have better cost economizing properties will eventually displace those that have worse, ceteris paribus" (Williamson 1981, p. 574). Overall, relationship quality affects relationship performance positively (Palmatier 2008).

Relationship Breadth The second driver of RM effectiveness, *relationship breadth*, represents the number of relational bonds with an exchange partner; interorganizational relationships that include many interpersonal ties can uncover key information, find profit-enhancing opportunities, and withstand disruptions to individual bonds (e.g., reorganizations, turnover). For example, broad interorganizational relationships recover more easily and suffer fewer long-lasting impacts from the departure of a key contact person (Bendapudi and Leone 2002). The replacement boundary spanner quickly becomes socialized into existing relational norms by those who remain with the firm through the process of "norm persistence" (Jacobs and Campbell 1961).

Interfirm relationships that include many interpersonal ties can uncover key information, find profit-enhancing opportunities, and withstand disruptions to individual bonds.

In addition, relationship breadth mirrors the network concepts of network density (i.e., level of interconnectedness among network members) and degree centrality (i.e., number of direct ties between a specific member and other network members) (Houston et al. 2004). Such network interconnections positively affect cooperation, knowledge transfer, communication efficiency, and product development performance (Rowley 1997; Tsai 2001; Walker, Kogut, and Shan 1997). That is, a seller and a customer that share more interpersonal ties (i.e., breadth) enjoy better access to information and sales opportunities and less disruption when contact personnel turn over, which then results in increased exchange performance (Palmatier 2008, 2007).

Relationship Composition *Relationship composition* refers to the decision-making capability of relational contacts; a diverse and authoritative contact portfolio increases a seller's ability to effect change in customer organizations. Greater diversity and authority mean the seller can triangulate its information across different perspectives and gain access to critical decision makers throughout the sales cycle (Katrichis 1998). For example, a new product approval process may progress through the customer's engineering, manufacturing, quality, and purchasing departments. A strong relationship with a vice president of purchasing has little impact when the product is sitting on a quality technician's bench; the relationship composition concept recognizes the limits of even high-quality relationships with multiple contacts (breadth) within the customer firm. If those relationships do not include key decision makers or apply only to similar types of positions, they cannot effect change. Relationship breadth and composition may correlate positively, since if all else is equal, sellers with more contacts have diverse contacts (horizontal and vertical diversification). However, these constructs may diverge if sellers have many homogeneous contacts or only a few very different contacts.

Overall, relationship composition captures the contact portfolio's aggregate ability to influence decisions by acknowledging that different areas within the customer firm make key decisions, not just those people with the most authority or "key" decision makers. For example, Arora and Allenby (1999, p. 476) empirically support the premise that "instead of exclusively focusing on the group members with a higher overall influence, it may be more beneficial to communicate to members who have lower overall influence but higher influence on specific aspects of the decision."

In this sense, relationship composition matches the network concepts of diversity (Wasserman and Faust 1994) and attractiveness (Anderson, Håkansson, and Johanson 1994), which entail the extent of unique knowledge, skills, and capabilities owned by network partners. Diverse network partners increase information value and complementarity (Burt 1992), as well as network performance and efficiency (Baum, Calabrese, and Silverman 2000). Despite the limited conceptual or empirical attention granted to relationship composition in RM literature, the underlying logic of its positive effect on performance is consistent with sales research pertaining to buying centers (Bonoma and Johnston 1978) and popular solution selling approaches (e.g., Rackham 1996), which suggest that a seller with a well-structured customer contact portfolio indeed has greater access to valuable, nonredundant information, can identify and overcome barriers, and therefore enjoys increased performance.

Alone, these three relational drivers capture different aspects of interfirm relationships. Together, they reinforce one another and promote optimum relationship value. That is, relationship quality has not only a direct effect on the seller's outcomes but also a conceptually meaningful, positive, leveraging effect through its interaction with relationship breadth and composition on performance outcomes.

Relationship Strength *Relationship strength* equals the interaction between relationship quality and relationship breadth, that is, an interorganizational relationship's ability to withstand stress and conflict, such that multiple high-quality relational bonds result in strong, resilient relationships. Due to this synergistic relationship between relationship quality and breadth, many cursory contacts (greater breadth, low quality) provide little protection against the stress of a service failure (e.g., poor delivery performance), because the low-quality contacts will not support the seller (lack of relational motivation). Similarly, a single high-quality contact (high quality, less breadth) will not risk being the sole supporter or perhaps cannot influence a decision-making group (Brown 2000). In contrast, multiple high-quality contacts (greater breadth, high quality) experience both relational motivation (commitment, norms of reciprocity) and confidence (trust) and therefore support the seller during a service recovery. As indirect support, service literature indicates that both relationship duration and breadth affect service recovery positively (Bejou and Palmer 1998; Hess,

Ganesan, and Klein 2003). In other words, relationship strength positively influences seller outcomes by increasing the interfirm relationship's ability to withstand problems and conflict while it continues to function effectively.

This conceptualization highlights an interesting parallel with engineering concepts. A bridge's strength and ability to withstand stress depends on the interaction of the quality and number of cables (i.e., quality × breadth) used to build the structure. Reporting only the quality of the cable without reporting the number of cables provides limited insight into the bridge's ability to withstand stress. Similarly, research that models interfirm relationship strength with just the quality of relational bonds (i.e., trust and commitment) will not provide a clear portrait of true relationship strength.

Relationship Efficacy Another interaction—relationship quality × relationship composition, or *relationship efficacy*—captures an interorganizational relationship's ability to achieve desired objectives. High-quality bonds in well-structured contact portfolios give sellers the means to execute their selling strategies effectively. For example, if a seller's contact portfolio contains key decision makers (high composition) but weak interpersonal bonds (low quality), the contacts will not disclose information (Crosby, Evans, and Cowles 1990) or care much about the seller's needs (reciprocity debts). More formally, relationship composition reflects the contact portfolio's latent ability to institute change; only high-quality relationships can turn this potential into reality and enable the seller to achieve its objectives (Anderson and Narus 1991; Morgan and Hunt 1994). In contrast, a portfolio might encompass high-quality, broad relationships, but it suffers if those contacts are restricted to one functional area with little decision-making ability (low composition) because the seller lacks access to divergent (nonredundant) information and cannot promote customer change. As network theory similarly notes, "It is critical to separate the issues of tie strength from that of network diversity," because "the most desirable ties are both *strong* and *diverse*" (Li 2007, p. 239); only when both exist is performance maximized. Rangan (2000, p. 826) also suggests synergy: "[A] large network of strong ties to nonredundant actors is the best sort to have."

The proposed impact of relationship efficacy parallels research on job seekers; relational ties increase a person's chances of landing a new job only when they connect him or her with someone "who is well placed in the occupational structure" (Granovetter 1983, p. 207). Thus, bonds with and the position of the contact together determine the effectiveness of the relationship in helping a seller achieve its objectives, and relationship efficacy positively affects seller per-

Figure 2
Model of Interfirm Relationship Marketing

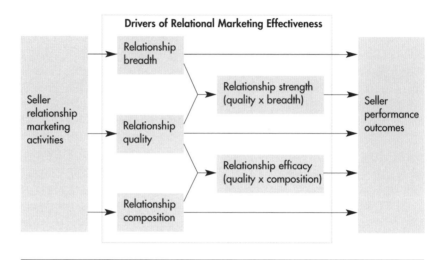

formance outcomes, because such contacts likely cooperate and reciprocate past favors when they experience high-quality relational bonds.

Overall, this model integrates social network theory to develop an interfirm-specific RM framework.[2] The framework clarifies that, in addition to relationship quality, two other relational drivers are key to understanding the impact of interfirm relationships on performance, namely, relationship breadth and composition. Furthermore, it recognizes the enhanced effects that emerge from the interactions of these drivers. Thus, the framework provides a direct representation of how RM investments affect seller outcomes because of the mediating mechanisms unique to interfirm relationships (see Figure 2).

Interpersonal Relationship Marketing Theory

Most theoretical and empirical RM research relies on models of interfirm relationships, which then extend to interpersonal or consumer research to suggest that the effects of RM on performance depend on some combination of trust and commitment (Crosby, Evans, and Cowles 1990; De Wulf, Odekerken-Schröder, and Iacobucci 2001; Garbarino and Johnson 1999; Sirdeshmukh,

Singh, and Sabol 2002).³ Such an application of social exchange theory entails several concerns. First, social exchange theory proposes that human relationships result from subjective cost–benefit analyses that attempt to maximize benefits and minimize costs, which may be more applicable in B2B contexts than in contexts involving intrapersonal dyads (i.e., more emotionally charged). Second, exchange theory often draws on reciprocity norms as an underlying building block (Gouldner 1960), but RM paradigms and models often ignore reciprocity, even though it (along with gratitude) likely represents a critical mediator of interpersonal RM. As Bagozzi (1995, p. 275) states, reciprocity sits "at the core of marketing relationships." Furthermore, the absence of a reciprocity measure for exchange partners in RM literature remains "especially notable" (Palmatier et al. 2006, p. 152). Despite the frequency with which reciprocity and gratitude (reciprocity's "emotional core") serve as conceptual explanations of RM outcomes, they virtually never appear or are measured in modern models or empirical analyses of relationship marketing (Becker 1986). This important gap leaves marketers unaware of a customer's reciprocity debt or feeling of gratitude. If a seller knows that a customer feels gratitude, that seller should attempt to sell additional products, up-sell higher priced products, or ask customers to participate in a time-consuming survey or training event before the feelings dissipate. Allowing a consumer to reciprocate a feeling of gratitude converts a short-term emotion into a long-lasting relational norm.

Allowing a consumer to reciprocate a feeling of gratitude converts a short-term emotion into a long-lasting relational norm.

According to evolutionary psychologists (Becker 1986; Trivers 1971; Trivers 1985), feelings of reciprocity and gratitude are genetically and socially hardwired into people, which makes their pervasiveness throughout societies reasonable; they represent the fundamental social and moral components for the functioning of stable social systems (Emmons and McCullough 2004; Gouldner 1960; Ostrom and Walker 2003). Relationship marketing assumes cyclical reciprocation: if I do something for you, I expect you to do something for me in return. In this context, gratitude is inseparable from reciprocity because it reflects an ingrained psychological pressure to return the favor. According to Becker (1986, p. 73), "People everywhere do 'feel' such obligations. . . . The mere recognition of benefit seems to generate a sense of obligation to repay." Reciprocal exchanges further represent a potent source of pleasure; people even feel inclined toward punishment if another partner fails to reciprocate.

However, relationship marketing goes beyond the short-term effects of gratitude; otherwise, customers could easily repay their debt and dismiss their obligation to the seller. Instead, because gratitude entails psychological pressure that leads to *social* conformity pressures, norms of reciprocity emerge and create persistent behavior cycles. That is, people engage in reciprocation cycles because they always have and because social norms support that action. Gratitude and reciprocity also operate at the lowest level (or below) of awareness (i.e., emotions and peer pressure), but social exchange theory focuses on "higher" cognitive processing levels. Some researchers argue that the two constructs actually help explain the effectiveness of relationship marketing (Palmatier et al. 2007b), such that including reciprocity and gratitude as mediators in the RM paradigm provides a "micro"-theoretical explanation of the underlying association between RM investments and outcomes. Interpersonal trust and commitment (e.g., relationship quality) mediate interpersonal relationships, just as they do interfirm relationships, but a true explanation of interpersonal RM effectiveness must include gratitude and norms of reciprocity, whereas relationship breadth and composition become largely irrelevant in dyadic interpersonal relationships. Figure 3 provides an overall conceptual model of interpersonal RM that encompasses the roles of consumer gratitude and norms of reciprocity; the next section further outlines their effects on short- and long-term returns on RM investments.

Role of Consumer Gratitude Because grateful people acknowledge how others have contributed to their well-being (Watkins et al. 2003), customer gratitude increases in response to favors (Goei and Boster 2005), and grateful customers reward firms for extra efforts (Morales 2005), such as by complying with subsequent requests (Goei and Boster 2005). According to retailing research, consumers satisfy their obligations to salespeople by purchasing (Dahl, Honea, and Manchanda 2005), which implies seller investments in RM make consumers feel grateful, which then prompts them to engage in behaviors that improve seller performance (Palmatier et al. 2007b).

However, the cognitively focused constructs of commitment and trust cannot be divorced from the emotional concept of gratitude. Cognition and emotion entwine closely, and (emotional) gratitude positively influences (cognitive) judgments of trust (Dunn and Schweitzer 2005). As Young (2006) posits, gratitude is a "relationship-sustaining" emotion with important implications for relational trust. Not only does gratitude enhance short-term consumer purchasing behaviors, it also promotes consumer trust and reciprocity norms with its longer-term effects (Palmatier et al. 2007b).

Figure 3
Model of Interpersonal Relationship Marketing

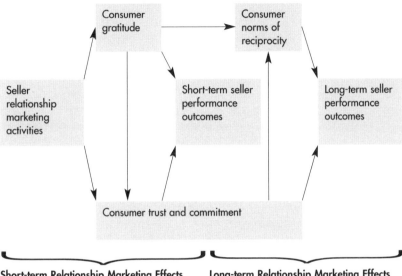

In this sense, gratitude represents a "starting mechanism" that influences prosocial behavior as long as the emotion lasts and then extends to longer-term effects because it *builds the relationship* (Bartlett and DeSteno 2006) by prompting norms of reciprocity in consumers' minds. Thus, gratitude initiates an ongoing cycle of reciprocation, which self-reinforces norms of reciprocity. Schwartz (1967, p. 8) highlights the gratitude–reciprocity cycle link by describing the "continuing balance of debt—now in the favor of one member, now in the favor of another," which guarantees relationship continuation because "gratitude will always constitute a part of the bond linking them."

Thus, gratitude enhances RM performance in three main ways:

1. Consumers engage in positive purchase behaviors to satisfy their feelings of obligation in response to RM-induced feelings of gratitude.

2. The increased levels of consumer trust, due to gratitude, increase consumer commitment and thus enhance relational performance outcomes.

3. Gratitude promotes the development of norms of reciprocity over the longer term and initiates a reciprocation cycle, which has long-term positive effects on consumer behaviors.

In summary, the positive returns on RM activities rely on gratitude as an underlying, supporting psychological mechanism (Palmatier et al. 2007b).

Role of Consumer Norms of Reciprocity Various studies in different contexts support the importance of reciprocity norms in decision processes. Dawson (1998) disentangles various motivations for donating to charities and highlights norms of reciprocity as a significant factor; Whatley and colleagues (1999) indicate that norms encourage compliance with requests to reciprocate, regardless of whether the consequences of that compliance are known; Diekmann (2004) reveals that norms of reciprocity shape altruistic cooperative behavior, even in high-stakes situations; and Cialdini and Rhoads (2001) identify reciprocity as one of six basic psychological principles that underlie successful influence tactics.

Social norms in general drive behaviors, as long as they are salient to the particular situation (Kallgren, Reno, and Cialdini 2000). Thus, norms of reciprocity are effective in an RM context because gratitude in response to relationship marketing triggers proper salience, which heightens the norm's influence on purchase decisions. Because consumer norms of reciprocity have such long-term, positive effects on consumer purchase behaviors, they also represent an important mechanism for understanding what makes RM activities successful.

This second, interpersonal model of RM integrates gratitude from psychology and norms of reciprocity from sociology to suggest a framework in which two relational drivers other than trust and commitment influence performance. This model (Figure 3, p. 29) also argues that RM is inherently dynamic, so different factors affect short- versus long-term performance.

Overall, gratitude and norms of reciprocity take a central role, in addition to trust and commitment, in interpersonal RM and thus help explain the strong empirical and managerial support for the impact of interpersonal relationships on decision making. That RM is an effective strategy for influencing consumer decision making is not surprising; its effect is supported by the underlying psychological emotion of gratitude, which leads to a desire to repay debt. The process of repaying generates feelings of pleasure, whereas the failure to do so generates feelings of guilt. In addition to a well-designed psychological system that causes consumers to repay RM investments, these same mechanisms result in strong social norms that reinforce consumers' compliance with RM efforts.

Relationship marketing's influence on decision making is supported by the underlying psychological emotion of gratitude, which leads to a desire to repay. The process of repaying generates feelings of pleasure, whereas the failure generates feelings of guilt.

The model of interfirm RM accounts for multiple interfirm relationships through relational quality (i.e., trust, commitment, and reciprocity norms), breadth, and composition; however, because each interfirm tie represents an interpersonal dyad, the model of interfirm relationship could be expanded by integrating gratitude and reciprocity into a multilevel RM model. For example, the ultimate outcome of interfirm exchanges results from both interpersonal-level decisions (based on dyadic trust, commitment, gratitude, and reciprocity norms) and group-level decisions (based on group-level relationship quality, breadth, and composition). A fully specified model of RM must account for each level and identify the conditions in which each plays a larger role in influencing exchange outcomes.

Multilevel Relationships

Relationships often develop and operate simultaneously at multiple levels within an exchange (see Figure 4). For example, individual customer decision makers can develop relationships with individual salespeople (interpersonal) and with the overall selling firm as an aggregate group (individual-to-firm), and a group of people at the customer can develop a relationship with a group of people at the seller (interfirm). All these relationships can influence customer purchase behaviors and outcomes. Thus, a key question emerges: how do multiple relationships simultaneously operate within an exchange to influence performance?

When relationships function at multiple levels, they also operate in multiple ways (Iacobucci and Ostrom 1996). According to Doney and Cannon (1997, p. 45), "[T]he processes by which trust develops appear to differ when the target is an organization . . . as opposed to an individual salesperson." Furthermore, empirical studies document that conceptually and empirically distinct constructs operate at interpersonal versus person-to-firm relationship levels (Crosby and Stephens 1987; Palmatier et al. 2007c; Palmatier, Scheer, and Steenkamp 2007; Sirdeshmukh, Singh, and Sabol 2002).

Figure 4
Multilevel Exchange Relationships

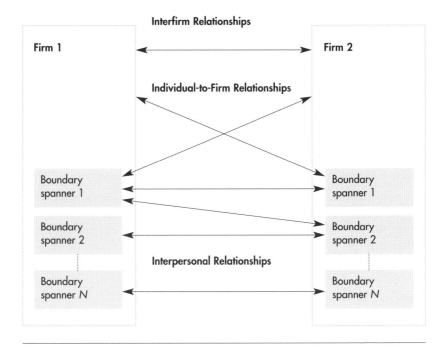

Depending on the relationship level or target (individual, group), different underlying processes influence the effects of RM on financial outcomes, according to social judgment theory (Hamilton and Sherman 1996; O'Laughlin and Malle 2002). For example, consumers' judgments about individual salespeople generally form differently than their judgments about the collective firm (Lickel et al. 2000), largely because of perceived differences in *entitativity*, or the degree to which a party exhibits coherence, unity, or consistency (Campbell 1958; Hilton and von Hippel 1990). Because consumers tend to attribute other individuals' actions to their stable, underlying characteristics, they judge those individuals on the basis of a well-elaborated, regularly updated, online model that integrates all available information, beginning with their first encounter. In contrast, groups generally lack entitativity (Hilton and von Hippel 1990; Menon et al. 1999), so consumers form their judgments about a firm using a less demanding, episodic recall model that weights recent and unusual behaviors more heavily. The former type of judgments based on an online model is much stronger and more confidently held. Therefore, even if judgments rely on the same behavioral information, "existing evidence reveals differences in the outcomes of impressions formed of individual and group targets" (Hamilton and Sherman 1996, p. 336).

In summary, all else being equal, relationships with individuals (e.g., salespeople) have a greater direct effect on relational behaviors and subsequent financial outcomes than do similar relationships with firms or groups of people. Individual-level relationships also have an indirect impact on outcomes because they affect the customer's relationship with the firm as a representative member of the firm. In addition, the impact of firm-level relationships on behavior and performance increases when customers perceive the firm's employees, policies, and procedures as consistent, since people treat very consistent groups as individual entities (Palmatier et al. 2007c; Palmatier, Scheer, and Steenkamp 2007).

Another important difference between individual- and firm-level relationships involves relational-induced loyalty, such that loyalty due to salesperson–customer relationships can be transient. If the salesperson leaves to join a competitive firm, he or she can take this loyalty along (Reichheld and Teal 1996). Empirical evidence reveals that "salesperson-owned loyalty, [and] the customer's intention to perform behaviors that signal motivation to maintain a relationship specifically with the focal salesperson" drives performance but is lost to the selling firm when the salesperson leaves the firm (Palmatier, Scheer, and Steenkamp 2007, p. 186). Thus, though individual-level relationships have a stronger impact on behaviors and outcomes, they also are more susceptible to disruption as a result of individual employee turnover (Bendapudi and Leone 2002). This is a real problem for some firms. For example, American Express reports that 30% of its customers would follow their relationship manager to a new firm (Tax and Brown 1998).

As loyalty to the firm is typically measured, the customer loyalty owned by the firm is mixed with the customer loyalty owned by the salesperson. Thus, customer loyalty can be decomposed into three parts. *Salesperson-owned loyalty*, the customer's intention to perform behaviors that signal motivation to maintain a relationship specifically with the focal salesperson; *seller-owned loyalty*, loyalty to the seller specifically, independent of the salesperson, that is based on elements the seller as an organization controls or in other employees of the seller with whom the customer interacts; and *synergistic loyalty*, loyalty engendered neither by the seller apart from the salesperson nor by the salesperson individually, but by the customer benefits the seller–salesperson association generates. Thus, a key issue in relationship marketing that must be considered is where the relationship resides and what actions can be taken to manage this process.

In addition, recent research investigating the impact of trust at three different levels within an international joint venture (Fang et al. 2008) shows that the interfirm relationship between parent companies, interpersonal trust among the parent firms' representatives, and the parent firms' trust in their own representatives (i.e., agency trust) have differential influences on resource investments and utilization and on the performance of the joint ventures. Moreover, these different levels of trust interact to increase coordination and suppress responsiveness among members of the joint venture. Thus, when investigating relationships among different entities with numerous constituents, a more nuanced view that accounts for relational ties among multiple constituents must be evaluated.

3

How Do Relationships Change over Time?

Few people would argue with the premise that relationships change over time and are dynamic, but most of academic research and managerial practice uses a static perspective to evaluate customer–seller relationships. This apparent contradiction stems mainly from the difficulty associated with capturing and analyzing relational data across time. For example, if a customer–seller relationship migrates through multiple stages in a relationship lifecycle over many years and most relational constructs are latent or unobserved (e.g., trust, gratitude), which requires customer self-reports, data collection efforts for a large portfolio of customers grow overwhelming. In practice, salespeople often use their emotional intelligence, adaptive selling, and empathy skills to gather observable relationship cues and thus track relational progress and adapt their selling behaviors accordingly. But when firms use multiple customer interfaces, minimize their use of direct selling to limit costs, and attempt to directly target individual customers, a dynamic understanding becomes more critical, because salespeople can no longer provide a single point of contact and use intuitive relational information and processes.

The question of how relationships change over time requires a two-part answer. First, extant literature claims that relationships are path dependent and progress through well-defined stages (i.e., lifecycle view), in which the role and linkage among relational constructs and performance outcomes vary across stages. Second, an emerging, dynamic view builds on the lifecycle perspective by considering the importance of the level, velocity, and acceleration of relational constructs for predicting exchange performance and relationship trajectories.

Relationship Lifecycle Stages

Many marketing researchers assume relationships operate according to a lifecycle process, during which they develop and ultimately dissolve by progressing through path-dependent stages. An exchange dyad's position on the relationship lifecycle can provide insight into how it will perform now and in the future. Table A1 (see Appendix) provides a summary of illustrative studies from marketing and management research that describe relationship dynamics and lifecycle effects and thus offers insight into how relational constructs operate across time and stages.

Drawing motivation from Arndt's (1979) discussion of "domesticated" markets, Dwyer, Schurr, and Oh (1987) brought the relationship development process (lifecycle) perspective to the fore by integrating insights from exchange theory (Hunt 1983; Thibaut and Kelley 1959) and modern contract law (Macneil 1980) to propose that successful interfirm relationships travel through four main stages, from awareness to commitment.

Most frameworks note that relationships begin with an *exploratory* or *identifying stage*, marked by limited confidence in the partner's ability and trustworthiness, as well as a willingness to explore the relationship because of perceptions of potential benefits that may exceed those available from alternative partners. During communications with such potential partners, the parties realize synergistic norms and goals in reciprocated transactions (Dwyer, Schurr, and Oh 1987; Hibbard et al. 2001; Jap and Ganesan 2000; Wilson 1995). Several studies note that initial levels of trust and commitment are calculative in nature, such that expectations of trustworthy behavior rely on the expectation that a partner will act in a manner that protects its reputation (Wilson 1995), enables it to avoid punishment from institutional enforcement mechanisms such as laws and regulations (Lewicki and Bunker 1996; Luna-Reyes, Cresswell, and Richardson 2004; Rousseau et al. 1998), and allows it to protect its bilateral investments (Jap and Ganesan 2000).

When initial experiences are positive and produce both desired outcomes and experiential evidence of trustworthiness (for a game-theoretic description of how trust develops through experience, see Boyle and Bonacich [1970]), relationships should grow during the *expansion* or *developing stage*. This growth includes an escalation of reciprocated transactions and increased affective attachment, as demonstrated in variables such as trust, commitment, and satisfaction.

If the relationship continues to the developing phase, the partners obtain increased benefits and greater interdependence, and then reach a *maturity, commitment*, or *maintaining stage*. Their calculative trust is replaced by knowledge-based (Rosseau et al. 1998) and affective-based trust, communication and other relational norms develop and reinforce their common goals, both firms believe their partner's behaviors are predictable, and mutual investments fall into place.

These factors combine to increase the partners' willingness to make long-term commitments to the relationship by committing irretrievable investments (Frazier 1983; Wilson 1995) and expressing their expectations of continued interactions (Dwyer, Schurr, and Oh 1987).

However, some research also suggests that previously successful relationships can enter a *negative* or *terminating stage* (e.g., "dissolution" [Dwyer, Schurr, and Oh 1987]; "decline" [Jap and Ganesan 2000]). Although Hibbard and colleagues (2001) do not label a particular phase, they note that the relationship between trust or commitment and performance declines over time. Such studies thereby describe the results of relationship dissatisfaction (Dwyer, Schurr, and Oh 1987) in which one party takes a shorter-term view and begins to explore alternative partners or approaches to terminate the existing relationship (Heide 1994; Jap and Ganesan 2000).

As relationships age, trust and commitment become less important in predicting performance.

In summary, these conceptual models suggest a common developmental process for relationships that follows a simple trajectory. Relational constructs, such as trust, commitment, and relational norms, develop and grow together as the relationships proceed, thus producing positive relational outcomes. In turn, when dissatisfaction shifts a relationship toward dissolution (e.g., because of poor performance, dependence concerns, or opportunistic betrayal), the relational mediators decline (Elangovan and Shapiro 1998). Thus, most conceptual research suggests relational constructs and outcomes march in lockstep (Ring and Van de Ven 1994).

A small body of empirical research into relationship phases also shows that relationships may differ qualitatively across phases (Grayson and Ambler 1999; Hibbard et al. 2001; Jap and Ganesan 2000). In both B2B (e.g., Grayson and Ambler 1999) and B2C (Mittal, Katrichas, and Kumar 2001) contexts, the empirical linkages between relational constructs and performance outcomes appear to vary across stages, though few theories explain why or how. For example, Hibbard and colleagues (2001) report trust and commitment become less important in predicting relationship performance as relationships age, and Moorman, Zaltman, and Deshpandé (1992) find that relational variables (including trust and commitment) cannot predict the adoption of market research services by client firms in later stages. Perhaps, they argue, relationship partnerships become "stale" over time, which diminishes objectivity, raises expectations, and increases opportunism. Grayson and Ambler (1999) respond to Moorman, Zaltman, and Deshpandé's (1992) claims by testing the link between relational constructs and performance outcomes moderated by relationship duration. In general, they find support for their expectations of a "dark side" of long-term relationships, though its exact nature remains rather unclear.

Most study designs adopt a cross-sectional perspective, categorizing relationships into phases on the basis of age (Grayson and Ambler 1999; Jap and Ganesan 2000) or including age as a covariate (Hibbard et al. 2001). In a recent review article on trust in interorganizational contexts, management scholars Lewicki, Tomlinson, and Gillespie (2006) argue that previous studies have been "static" and that longitudinal examinations of individual relationships remain noticeably absent. Thus, further research is needed to clarify how well the relationship lifecycle view matches reality, as well as whether the specific stages capture meaningful transition points. However, initial evidence appears to suggest that the levels of various relationship constructs (e.g., trust, commitment) lose their predictive power as a relationship moves into its later stages.

Dynamic View of Relationships

Inconsistencies in the lifecycle perspective of relationships suggest that relationships need to be investigated within a more dynamic framework. Recent research has started to address this need by using latent growth curve modeling to study the time-varying trajectories of constructs across sociology, psychology, and marketing (Bollen and Curran 2006; Palmatier et al. 2007a). Latent growth curve analysis investigates the developmental or growth process of constructs by modeling the level, velocity, and acceleration factors (latent growth parameters) that explain the observed growth trajectories. In this sense, it offers support for investigations into the antecedents and outcomes of these growth factors. Although exploratory, findings from such analyses provide interesting insights into the dynamic nature of relationships.

For example, in one study trust increases during the first six years (see Figure 5), but commitment peaks at about year four and then starts to decay (Palmatier et al. 2007a). Thus, trust and commitment do not follow the same lifecycle or growth trajectory but rather diverge as the relationship ages. Furthermore, these constructs appear dynamically linked, such that the initial level of trust positively influences the initial level of commitment, but the velocity of trust also positively influences the velocity of commitment. Thus, factors

Figure 5
Interfirm Relationship Lifecycle: Role of Relational Velocity

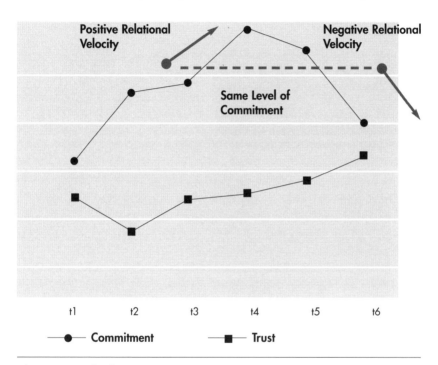

Palmatier, Dant, Grewal, and Houston 2007a

that increase the growth rate of trust provide value by increasing the growth rate of commitment (i.e., building the relationship faster) and postponing the point at which commitment peaks and the relationship begins to decay (i.e., extending the life of the relationship).

However, only the velocity and acceleration of commitment exert significant positive effects on exchange performance (e.g., sales growth); surprisingly, the effect of the level of commitment on sales growth is not significant. Thus, the *level* of commitment (as typically measured in cross-sectional research), in isolation, provides little insight into the future of the relationship because it ignores the trajectory of the relational mediators and the position of the relationship on its overall trajectory. If commitment starts high but has begun to decay, a static measurement would capture higher commitment than it would for another relationship with lower starting levels that have yet to peak. In this way, investigating only the level of commitment can provide terribly misleading predictions. This finding is consistent with that of Jap and Anderson (2007, p. 271) who note that "for the most part, maturity is never better than build-up and is often marginally inferior." That is, the direction and rate of change in relational constructs (at least for commitment) provide crucial information for explaining and predicting relational outcomes. For example, in Figure 5 the dotted line intersects the curve representing commitment at the same *level* at two points in time, but evaluating the *velocity* of commitment (slopes) provides critical insight into the future of the relationship and its impact on performance.

An important implication is that key information is captured not so much in the stage of lifecycle as in the trajectory or relationship dynamics (i.e., velocity and acceleration). The trajectory of trust only influences outcomes via its effect on commitment. Another implication is that low levels of initial trust and/or commitment in a relationship may be overcome by higher levels of velocity and/or acceleration. In other words, a "rocky" start does not necessarily mean a relationship is doomed. Thus, research could incorporate dynamic variables into studies on relationship recovery.

A "rocky" start does not necessarily mean a relationship is doomed: low levels of trust and/or commitment may be overcome by high levels of relational velocity.

Overall, this emerging view suggests that relationships are much more dynamic than their typical conceptualization and operationalization would imply. In other words, models linking RM strategies → relational constructs → performance appear to vary across development stages, suggesting that relationship stage or dynamics need to be integrated into relationship marketing strategy. Those RM strategies that are most effective in early stages may not work later. A focus on growing rather than maintaining relationships may represent a critical success factor to relationship marketing; "relationship maintenance" not only precedes decline but also represents a poorly performing relationship state, which suggests it should be actively avoided.

An Applied Perspective of Relationship Marketing

4

Understanding Relationship Marketing's Financial Impact

Managers expend time and money on relationship marketing, believing that it ultimately leads to improved financial performance, but as with other marketing programs (e.g., advertising, tradeshows, public relations), capturing the actual financial impact of specific programs or isolating the mechanisms through which performance improves is rather difficult. This chapter explores the financial impact of RM in two parts. The first part examines RM's influence on financial performance in multiple causal stages: RM activities → relational assets → relational behaviors → financial outcomes (see Figure 6). The framework also features specific performance-enhancing relational behaviors or mechanisms, including increased cooperation, loyalty, referrals or word-of-mouth, and empathetic behaviors, that represent researchers' most common explanations for the influence of relationships on firms' financial performance.

The second part summarizes how to measure relational assets and the research that links them to financial outcomes, because an important aspect of RM deals with managing relational assets.

Linking Relationship Marketing to Financial Outcomes

Relationship marketing activities likely do not affect financial performance directly but rather help build and/or maintain customer–seller relationships (i.e., relational assets), which then influence customer behaviors, which in turn generate improvements in the seller's financial outcomes (Figure 6). This causal chain is valid for both individual customers and the seller's overall portfolio of customers, depending on the scope of analysis. Next, each of these causal steps is discussed briefly.

The impact of RM on performance goes through four stages: RM activities → relational assets → relational behaviors → financial outcomes.

Figure 6

Linking Relationship Marketing to Financial Outcomes

Relationship Marketing Activities

Relationship Marketing Programs

■ Social
■ Structural
■ Financial

Organizational Elements and Business Processes

■ Culture and climate
■ Leadership
■ Organizational structure
■ Business strategy
■ Compensation and control processes
■ Conflict resolution processes
■ Expertise
■ Frequency
■ Communication
■ Similarity

Relational Assets

Relationship Quality

■ Trust
■ Commitment
■ Reciprocity norms
■ Gratitude

Relationship Dynamics

■ Relational velocity
■ Age or lifecycle stage

Interfirm Relationships

■ Relationship breadth
■ Relationship composition
■ Relationship strength
■ Relationship efficacy
■ Relationship ownership

Relationship Marketing Activities Relationship marketing activities consist of dedicated RM programs, designed and implemented to build and maintain strong customer–seller relational bonds. These dedicated programs often are subdivided into social, structural, or financial programs. In addition to RM programs, other organizational elements and business processes of sellers may have important effects on the development, maintenance, or dissolution of customer–seller relational bonds. For example, social RM programs—taking a client to a sporting event or dinner—could be undermined if the salesperson is

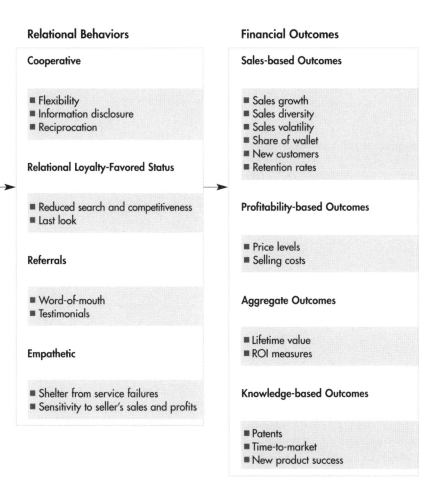

Relational Behaviors	Financial Outcomes
Cooperative	**Sales-based Outcomes**
■ Flexibility ■ Information disclosure ■ Reciprocation	■ Sales growth ■ Sales diversity ■ Sales volatility ■ Share of wallet ■ New customers ■ Retention rates
Relational Loyalty-Favored Status	**Profitability-based Outcomes**
■ Reduced search and competitiveness ■ Last look	■ Price levels ■ Selling costs
Referrals	**Aggregate Outcomes**
■ Word-of-mouth ■ Testimonials	■ Lifetime value ■ ROI measures
Empathetic	**Knowledge-based Outcomes**
■ Shelter from service failures ■ Sensitivity to seller's sales and profits	■ Patents ■ Time-to-market ■ New product success

incompetent or the firm fails to communicate changes in its delivery and order policies.

Relational Assets Both RM programs and the relationship-salient aspects of a firm's business influence sellers' relational assets. Such relational assets might be evaluated for either an individual customer or a portfolio of customers. In particular, relational assets capture the relational quality of the customer's bonds with the seller (i.e., trust, commitment, reciprocity norms, gratitude), the dynamics of the relationship (i.e., relational velocity, relationship age, or life-cycle stage), and, in the case of interfirm relationships, the characteristics of the relationship with the customer firm (i.e., relationship breadth, composition). That is, *relational assets* reflect the incremental, typically intangible value that a firm receives from its relational bonds with a customer or portfolio of customers. As outlined in the previous chapters regarding the theory of interfirm and interpersonal relationships, RM can change the nature of the relational bonds in various ways. These intangible relational assets influence a wide range of customers' behaviors and typically have a positive effect on sellers' financial performance.

Relational Behaviors Relational assets influence customer decision processes and behaviors in a multitude of ways, though most relationship-induced behaviors can be grouped into four major pathways or mechanisms. First, strong relationships increase customers' *cooperative behaviors*, the coordinated, complementary actions between partners to achieve a mutual goal. Such cooperation increases customers' willingness to be flexible and adapt to the seller's requests for changes, to share and disclose information to the seller, and to reciprocate the seller's efforts over the life of the exchange. Cooperation also promotes value creation beyond what each firm could achieve separately, but because one party often receives its portion of the value first, the other party must have enough trust in the relationship to wait for future reciprocation (Anderson and Narus 1990). This demand emerges especially when the party suffers significant risk while waiting for reciprocation. In the absence of trust, the range of cooperative behaviors likely is limited to those in which both parties receive their benefits simultaneously. Committed customers, by definition, want to maintain valued relationships, so they cooperate with sellers even in the absence of a *quid pro quo* benefit to strengthen and maintain their important customer–seller bond (Morgan and Hunt 1994). Research shows that trust, commitment, and relationship quality between exchange partners are critical for cooperation (Anderson and Narus 1990; Bettencourt 1997; Hewett and Bearden 2001; Palmatier et al. 2006).

Second, customers offer their seller partners *relational loyalty* or *favored status*, defined as the likelihood that the customer provides the seller with an advantage or benefits in the exchange process because of relational ties. These advantages might mean the customer engages in a limited search for alternatives, rebuys without soliciting competitive bids, or discloses competitive quotes so the favored seller can have a final opportunity to win the business (i.e., last look). Increased customer loyalty represents one of the most anticipated outcomes of RM efforts, but loyalty can be defined and measured in a plethora of ways (Jacoby and Chestnut 1978; Oliver 1999). Some studies focus on behavioral intentions (e.g., repurchase intentions, expectation of continuity), but these measures often suffer unduly from situational influences (Dick and Basu 1994; Jacoby and Chestnut 1978). For example, customers with weak relational bonds and little "ultimate loyalty" may report their high expectation of relationship continuity simply because of high switching costs, a lack of time to evaluate alternatives, or plain laziness (Oliver 1999). Even customers with strong relational bonds may lack total control over purchases or need to end a relationship prematurely because of unforeseen conditions. Thus, in some situations, behavioral intentions have limited influence on the seller's actual financial outcomes. In contrast, relationship-induced loyalty or favored status focuses on customer behaviors caused by relational bonds, not transaction inertia. Customers' commitment, trust, and relationship quality with a seller positively influence their loyalty, because they perceive less risk in dealing with trusted partners, act on relationally generated belonging, and minimize acquisition costs by buying from valued sellers (Doney and Cannon 1997; Garbarino and Johnson 1999; Hewett, Money, and Sharma 2002; Macintosh and Lockshin 1997).

Third, relational bonds represent the primary drivers of customer motivation and willingness to provide requested or unrequested referrals and testimonials (Barksdale, Johnson, and Suh 1997; Hennig-Thurau, Gwinner, and Gremler 2002; Verhoef, Franses, and Hoekstra 2002). The reduced cost and increased availability and use of Internet referrals make such behavior even more significant. Researchers define *referrals* or *word-of-mouth* (WOM) as the likelihood that a customer comments positively about a seller to another potential customer (whether inside or outside the firm). Because WOM behaviors are not masked by high switching costs and lack of time or motivation, they often appear as effective indicators of customer loyalty (Dick and Basu 1994; Reynolds and Beatty 1999), with the assumption that only customers with strong and trusting relationships risk their reputations by advocating a seller to another potential customer (Reichheld 2003). Thus, trust and commitment positively affect a customer's WOM behaviors (Barksdale, Johnson, and Suh 1997; Hennig-Thurau, Gwinner, and Gremler 2002; Verhoef, Franses, and Hoekstra 2002). However, the framework separates referrals and WOM behaviors from loyalty-favored status behaviors because they represent different performance-enhancing relational pathways. Loyalty affects financial outcomes by altering the exchange process *with the loyal customer*, whereas referrals often affect financial outcomes by *generating business with new customers*.

Fourth, customers display more *empathetic behaviors*, a greater likelihood to be influenced by their perceptions of the seller's exchange position, when the exchange is embedded in a strong relationship. Therefore, customers may attribute service failures to external causes that the seller cannot control, which reduces the impact of a failure on purchase behaviors. In addition, customers' enhanced sensitivity to the seller's position or hardships (e.g., offshore competition, reduced sales and profits) likely prompts them to minimize price-reduction pressures. Little extant research explores relational-induced empathetic behaviors and their impact on financial outcomes.

Financial Outcomes The last stage in the causal chain linking RM to financial performance involves financial performance metrics (seller-focal), which are influenced by the customer's relational behaviors and generally consist of four categories. The most common metrics, *sales-based outcome measures*, recognize that relational behaviors (e.g., reciprocation, reduced search, last look) can increase or minimize drops in sales revenue. Sales-based outcome measures take many forms, including annual sales growth, sales diversity (number of different products and services sold to a customer), sales volatility (variability in sales over time), and share of wallet (sales penetration for a specific customer). Some sales-based metrics are relevant only for a portfolio of customers, such as the number of new customers generated or retention and churn rates (firm's ability to retain existing customers). Although some relational behaviors indirectly affect sales, they may have a more direct impact on the seller's profit levels with customers (e.g., price premium).

Profitability-based outcome measures include price premiums (e.g., percentage a customer will pay to deal with a seller with which he or she has a strong relationship) and reduced selling costs. The diverse mechanisms by which RM can affect performance imply that *aggregate measures of performance* are best, because measuring sales alone probably provides an incomplete picture of the true effect of RM. For example, using *customer lifetime value* (CLV)–based measures captures the broad range of potential performance-enhancing relational behaviors because it discounts future cash flows and selling costs and thereby indicates the customer's present value (i.e., both sales and profit effects). Many argue that CLV represents the best overall measure of customer value and should guide most marketing actions, but in practice, it is difficult to capture the required data to make such calculations and often is very sensitive to assumptions (margins, future growth rates, allocation of costs). Another aggregate outcome measure well suited for evaluating specific marketing programs, as compared with customers, is return on investment (ROI). Research evaluating ROI in social, structural, and financial RM programs returns mixed results, in which social programs generate positive returns, structural programs break even in the first year, and financial programs fail to generate positive returns in the short term (Palmatier, Gopalakrishna, and Houston 2006).

The final group of outcome measures, *knowledge-based outcomes*, is not a true financial measure but may represent an important outcome of strong customer–seller relationships not captured by pure financial measures. Because customer relational behaviors may provide sellers with insight into new markets, help them uncover new product opportunities, enable them to beta test and refine new product concepts, and accelerate adoption of new product launches, strong relationships also may influence sellers' financial performance in ways that typical financial metrics cannot isolate (at least in the short run). These effects are especially difficult to capture because they occur displaced in both time and location from the customer's relational behaviors. For example, a customer may disclose critical information used by a seller to develop a proprietary new product, which generates profitable sales to different customers in different markets many years in the future. Linking RM investments in current customers to different future customers often represents an insurmountable problem. Instead, tracking an intermediate, knowledge-based outcome provides some indication of the ultimate effect of relational behaviors on future financial outcomes. Knowledge-based outcomes, such as number of patents, time to market, and new product success rate, also may provide insights into some relational benefits not captured in financial measures. Measuring knowledge-based outcomes may be especially important for firms implementing innovation-based strategies.

Relational assets influence customer decisions and behaviors through four pathways: cooperation, relational loyalty, referral, and empathetic behaviors.

Measuring Relationships and Financial Impact

The primary focus of RM—building and maintaining a firm's relational assets—relies on the belief that intangible assets generate positive financial outcomes in excess of their costs. Two important questions are embedded in this argument: (1) How do we measure a seller's relational assets? and (2) What empirical evidence supports the assumed positive linkage between relational assets and financial outcomes?

Measuring Relational Assets   Researchers and managers interested in the effects of customer relationships propose many different aspects as key to understanding the impact on performance and then offer multitudinous constructs and measures to capture the essence of relationships. Commitment and trust are the most often evaluated. Some researchers investigate commitment and trust individually as key constructs for predicting performance (i.e., Gundlach, Achrol, and Mentzer 1995; Sirdeshmukh, Singh, and Sabol 2002), whereas others suggest they influence different outcomes (Morgan and Hunt 1994) or merely indicate a global measure of relationship quality (Crosby, Evans, and Cowles 1990; De Wulf, Odekerken-Schröder, and Iacobucci 2001). For example, Doney and Cannon (1997, p. 35) observe that "trust has assumed a central role in the development of marketing theory"; in services, Berry (1996, p. 42) offers "trust as perhaps the single most powerful relationship marketing tool available to a company"; and Spekman (1988, p. 79) suggests that trust is the "cornerstone" of long-term relationships. Alternatively, Gundlach, Achrol, and Mentzer (1995, p. 78) propose commitment as the "essential ingredient for successful long-term relationships"; after reviewing multiple literature streams, Morgan and Hunt (1994, p. 23) suggest "commitment among exchange partners as key to achieving valuable outcomes." More recently, De Wulf, Odekerken-Schröder, and Iacobucci (2001, p. 36) report, "[W]e prefer the abstract relationship quality construct over its more specific dimensions because, even though these various forms of attitude may be conceptually distinct, consumers have difficulty making fine distinctions between them and tend to lump them together." A meta-analysis of two decades of RM research reveals compelling evidence for using a composite measure of relational quality, because no single or best relational mediator can capture the full essence or depth of a customer–seller relationship (Hennig-Thurau, Gwinner, and Gremler 2002; Johnson 1999; Palmatier et al. 2006). Moreover, relationship quality, a composite construct, predicts objective measures of a seller's financial performance significantly better than any single relational measure (Palmatier et al. 2006).

Researchers vary the relational aspects they include in their conceptualization of relational quality. Trust, commitment, reciprocity norms, and gratitude, though related, appear to capture unique features of the relational bond that positively influences specific exchange behaviors, but in aggregate, they indicate the overall quality or caliber of the bond. Table A2 (see Appendix) provides a summary of the constructs, definitions, and example items for some of the many measures of relational assets.

A static measure of relational quality provides a snapshot of the caliber of the relational bonds or ties, but understanding how the relationship changes or its relational velocity provides additional information about future exchange performance. For example, an exchange featuring a high level of relational quality that has peaked and is starting to decay (negative relational velocity) should perform worse in the future than another exchange with the same level of relational quality that is still strengthening (positive relational velocity) (see Figure 5, p. 39). Relational velocity might be measured in different ways. If a firm measures its relational quality annually, relational velocity can be determined from the annual rate of change. Alternatively, direct measures of relational velocity or the relationship lifecycle stage can help determine the direction and rate of change in the customer–seller relationship. In summary, high-caliber, growing relationships represent more valuable relational assets with stronger effects on seller financial outcomes than do lower caliber, stagnating, or decaying relationships.

Although relationship quality and velocity are key to both interpersonal and interfirm relationships, interfirm relationships often encompass relational bonds among multiple persons on both side of the exchange dyad. Thus, other aspects of interfirm relationships must be considered to evaluate the value of a relational asset. In this context, relationship breadth (number of relational ties with exchange partner) and relationship composition (decision-making capability of the relational contacts) capture important performance-enhancing information, because an interfirm relationship built on the basis of many interpersonal relationships with important decision makers is more valuable than an interfirm relationship based on only one interpersonal tie with a low-level contact.

Relationship strength (capacity or ability to withstand stress and/or conflict) and relationship efficacy (capacity or ability to achieve desired objectives) represent two other aspects of interfirm relationships. These aggregate constructs can be measured directly or derived from constituent constructs. For example, relationship strength represents the interaction of relationship quality and breadth, and relationship efficacy represents the interaction of relationship quality and composition. Alternatively, the direct measures in Table A2 (see Appendix) could be employed instead.

Relationship target and respondent versus informant issues Effectively measuring and understanding the impact of relational assets requires clearly defining the target of the relational measure. For example, when asking a customer to report on the quality of his or her relationship with a seller, the researcher must ensure each measure clearly specifies if the relationship target is the selling firm, an aggregate entity, or the primary sales contact or salesperson. Leaving the target of the relationship ambiguous may cause each measure to vary, depending on the degree to which it represents an individual- versus firm-level relationship. As discussed previously, individual-level relationships are less stable over time (e.g., due to job changes) but typically have a greater impact on customer behavior and financial outcomes. Thus, depending on the target of the relationship measure, these results will vary.

In addition to ensuring that each measurement item clearly defines the relationship target, researchers must design items such that customers completing relational measures report on either their own relationship with the target (i.e., acting as a respondent) or their evaluation of the relationship between some clearly defined entity and the target (i.e., acting as an informant). When using informants to report on relationships other than their own, researchers must take care to ensure the informants are knowledgeable and able to report on the relationship being investigated (e.g., between two firms). In many cases, it is advisable to ask supplementary questions to determine whether the informant has sufficient knowledge to answer the questions reliably or combine responses from multiple informants for dense interfirm relationships.

Effect of Relational Assets on Financial Outcomes   Most empirical research tests only a portion of the overall model linking RM investments to financial outcomes (Figure 6, p. 44) or uses nonfinancial outcomes (e.g., behavioral intentions, loyalty). However, different approaches have been used to provide insight into the financial returns of RM efforts; three of these are reviewed next.

Relationship duration approach   Some research, assuming that RM efforts result in longer relationship duration, investigates the impact of relationship duration on financial outcomes. Reinartz and Kumar (2000) consider the impact of relationship duration on customer profitability and show, as expected, that long-term customers represent most of a firm's profits, but short-term customers are also important in that they capture nearly 30% of the firm's profits. In most cases, relationship duration does not appear to be a strong predictor of customer profits or prices. Kalwani and Narayandas (1995) use secondary data to compare multiple performance outcomes for firms with long-term (> 6 years) versus shorter-term customers. Suppliers with longer-term customers achieve higher sales growth, inventory turnover, and return on invested capital but lower gross margins. Thus, though this research does not directly address the financial impact of relational assets, it suggests that relationship duration is a mixed predictor of relationship performance, perhaps because it fails to discriminate long-term customers whose relationship continues to expand (positive relational velocity) from those that have peaked, offer little growth, or are beginning to decline.

Relationship duration is a poor predictor of relationship performance, perhaps because it fails to discriminate growing relationships from those that are beginning to decline.

Lifetime value approach Many researchers attempt to isolate the overall financial value of customers, not just the value generated from relationships, using a customer lifetime value (CLV) approach. This method uses the discounted cash flow of a customer's purchases and models the customer's value according to the margin, marketing costs, purchase frequency, expected duration, and discount rates (Berger and Nasr 1998; Rust, Zeithaml, and Lemon 2000). Venkatesan and Kumar (2004) offer one of the most complete and sophisticated models of CLV, with which they investigate a range of antecedents of purchase frequency and margins to identify CLV drivers. They employ data that can be extracted from comprehensive B2B databases. Overall, they find that marketing actions (e.g., direct mailings, reward programs) positively affect pricing, purchase frequency, loyalty, and overall CLV. Rust, Lemon, and Zeithaml (2004) extend this approach by modeling an individual customer's lifetime value (customer equity) for a specific firm's brand by demonstrating the important role of customer perceptions and attitudes (e.g., quality, price, convenience, preferential treatment) in driving CLV. In summary, CLV uses prior customer behaviors that are visible to sellers to model a customer's value in the future; though a powerful approach, it often does not isolate the portion of CLV due to relational assets, so the impact of relationships on CLV may be overwhelmed by nonrelational factors (e.g., brand equity, innovative or proprietary products).

Return on investments and contribution margin Other approaches attempt to capture the incremental return generated from RM investments or relational assets to provide an indication of the ROI or returns on relationship marketing. Palmatier, Gopalakrishna, and Houston (2006) conduct an end-to-end study linking investments with three types of RM programs (social, structural, and financial) and measure the incremental profits generated to provide an indication of the ROI of RM programs. The results suggest that in the short term, social programs have the highest payoff, structural programs break even, and financial programs fail to pay off.

Palmatier (2007, 2008) also applies this approach in a B2B context to capture customer relational value (CRV) and isolate the value due to customers' relational assets; he finds that relationship quality, breadth, and composition all

In the short term, social programs have the highest payoff, structural programs break even, and financial programs fail to pay off.

influence CRV. Previous research proposing that the performance-enhancing effects of interfirm relationships can be captured fully by relationship quality, trust, or commitment therefore may be omitting important relationship aspects. For example, the extant relational paradigm predicts similar relationship benefits for two suppliers with similar levels of customer trust and commitment. But what if one supplier engages in an interfirm relationship that remains isolated to a few contacts in purchasing, whereas the other enjoys a multitude of contacts across many departments and levels? In this extreme case, most people would predict performance differences across the two suppliers, which intuitively supports the need to account for other relational drivers.

Overall, research focused on the financial return from relationship marketing investments and the value generated from relational assets provides a mixed picture. The findings are consistent, in that customer–seller relationships help determine the seller's financial performance, and RM investments can pay off in both short- and long-term financial returns. But not surprisingly, positive returns are not guaranteed, and the effects of relationships on behavior and exchange interactions are both ubiquitous and complex, which makes actual returns difficult to determine. Aggravating the inability of managers to identify effective RM strategies, returns depend on the type of RM programs and specific customer characteristics. In aggregate, these factors leave managers in a quandary: they know that building strong relationships is important, but they have little guidance on how to *build and maintain* strong customer relationships or *target and adapt their RM strategies* on the basis of customer and environmental factors. The next two chapters focus on these managerially crucial questions.

5
Building and Maintaining Strong Relationships

Arguably the most important issue facing managers who want to implement RM strategies is how to build and maintain strong relationships. This chapter addresses these questions in three parts. First, by summarizing prior empirical research, it provides insights into relationship drivers by focusing on the first causal linkage outlined in Figure 6, p. 44 (relationship marketing activities → relational assets). In other words, this section identifies the factors that have the greatest impact on customer–seller relationships, though these factors are limited to variables that have been studied previously.

Many factors affect a firm's success in building and maintaining strong customer relationships, but firms often focus most of their relational investments on dedicated RM programs. This choice is not surprising; marketing departments often treat RM as another form of promotion and employ the same structure and processes developed for traditional advertising or direct marketing campaigns. Moreover, implementing specific RM programs supports budgeting and evaluating program effectiveness (e.g., ROI) and typically can be managed within the marketing organization. In contrast, changes in firm-level culture, boundary-spanner personnel or training, marketing channels, and other customer-interfacing business processes are more difficult and riskier to implement. Thus, RM activities consist of two broad groups of activities: relationship marketing programs and other organizational elements and processes.

Second, this chapter narrows the focus to investigate the effects of different types of RM programs. More specifically, a review of academic research and popular practice provides a typology of RM programs for evaluating the efficacy of each type of program. Third, this chapter describes how a firm's organizational elements and business processes affect its ability to build and maintain strong customer–seller relationships.

Drivers of Customer Relationships

Meta-Analysis of Drivers[4] The many empirical articles studying the factors that lead to strong relationships support an empirical synthesis of such research. Palmatier et al. (2006) search the empirical research from 1987 to 2004 (17 years) and conduct a meta-analysis through which they identify 97 different empirical investigations representing 38,077 different relationships. By empirically combining the investigations and correcting for sample size and measurement errors, they clarify the most effective drivers of relationships, without depending on any one researcher, industry, or measurement method, which increases confidence in the robustness of the results. However, this approach can only synthesize factors that have already been studied, which means relatively new measures or variables (e.g., relationship breadth, composition) do not appear in their meta-analysis. The results of this meta-analysis are summarized in Table 3, starting with the drivers with the greatest impact on relational assets. The table clearly shows that not all relational drivers have an equal effect on relational assets; the average sample weighted reliability-adjusted correlations among drivers and relational asset is .41, ranging from .13 for relationship duration to the largest absolute effect of −.67 for conflict (correlations of 1 reflect perfectly correlated variables).

The evaluation of the relative impact of different RM strategies on building strong customer relationships indicates several insights. For example, conflict, defined as the overall level of disagreement between exchange partners and often termed perceived or manifest conflict (Gaski 1984), demonstrates the greatest impact on relational assets and destroys all aspects of relationship quality (trust, commitment, etc.) equally. Thus, partners must resolve problems and disagreements to prevent potentially corrosive, relationship-damaging disagreements. Customer confidence in the long-term orientation of the seller, as well as customer willingness to invest in relationship building or maintenance, declines with greater conflict, which implies that conflict negatively influences trust and commitment toward the seller (Anderson and Weitz 1992; MacKenzie and Hardy 1996). However, functional conflict refers to an amicable resolution of disagreements and represents a positive outcome of trust (Morgan and Hunt 1994). Exchange partners with strong relationships who disagree should be able to cooperate and find a mutually acceptable solution; if they cannot, the unresolved disagreements may fester and undermine the relationship. Finally, the largest effect in the meta-analysis is negative; consistent with other research, people apparently pay more attention to negatives than to positives in the RM

Table 3
Drivers of Relational Assets[1]

Relational Driver	Definitions	Adjusted r Between Relational Drivers and Relational Assets
Conflict	Overall level of disagreement between exchange partners	−.67
Seller expertise	Knowledge, experience, and overall competency of seller	.62
Communication	Amount, frequency, and quality of information shared between exchange partners	.54
Relationship investments	Seller's investment of time, effort, spending, and resources focused on building a stronger relationship	.46
Similarity	Commonality in appearance, lifestyle, and status between individual boundary spanners or similar cultures, values, and goals between buying and selling organizations	.44
Relationship benefits	Benefits received, including time saving, convenience, companionship, and improved decision making	.42
Dependence on seller	Customer's evaluation of the value of seller-provided resources for which few alternatives are available from other sellers	.26
Interaction frequency	Number of interactions or number of interactions per unit of time between exchange partners	.16
Relationship duration	Length of time that the relationship between the exchange partners has existed	.13

1. The results in this table are based on the meta-analysis performed by Palmatier et al. (2006).

domain (Fiske 1980; Shiv, Edell, and Payne 1997), and even hard-won relationships can suffer great damage because of conflict.

People pay more attention to negatives than to positives in RM; even hard-won relationships can suffer great damage because of conflict.

Yet positive influences emerge from the meta-analysis as well. For example, when a customer perceives a seller as more knowledgeable or credible (i.e., *seller expertise*), the information the seller provides seems more reliable, valuable, and persuasive (Dholakia and Sternthal 1977). As a result of the increased value of interacting with a competent seller, the customer finds the exchange relationship more important and invests more effort in strengthening and maintaining it (Lagace, Dahlstrom, and Gassenheimer 1991). Consistent with Vargo and Lusch's (2004, p. 3) premise that "skills and knowledge are the fundamental unit of exchange," seller expertise has the greatest positive impact of all antecedents across all forms of relationship quality (Palmatier et al. 2006). Because sellers' skill and knowledge, or expertise, provide the most important value-creating attributes, firms must train boundary spanners well, because inexperienced or unskilled employees can have seriously detrimental impacts.

Communication, or the amount, frequency, and quality of information shared between exchange partners (Mohr, Fisher, and Nevin 1996), also reveals a positive effect. Unlike unilateral forms of information exchange, such as disclosure or openness, bilateral communication builds stronger relationships by helping resolve disputes, align goals and expectations, and uncover new value-creating opportunities (Anderson and Narus 1990; Mohr and Nevin 1990; Morgan and Hunt 1994). Informativeness and clarity in exchanges improve relationship trust by giving both parties confidence in promises, and the identification of new value-creating opportunities increases relationship commitment. Consistent with its role in both uncovering value-creating opportunities and resolving conflict, communication indicates a significant positive effect on all aspects of relationship quality in the meta-analysis.

Relationship investment, similarity, and relationship benefits rank as the three next most influential antecedents of strong relationships. Relationship investment and benefits logically relate: by investing time, effort, expenditures, and resources, sellers build stronger relationships, which generate benefits such as time savings, convenience, companionship, and improved decision making. Investments could take the form of gifts, direct mailings, preferential treatment, or loyalty programs, and when relationship investments are irrecoverable, the ensuing psychological bonds and reciprocity expectations help strengthen and maintain the relationship (De Wulf, Odekerken-Schröder, and Iacobucci 2001; Smith and Barclay 1997). Furthermore, when customers receive benefits from the investments, they should perceive underlying relationship value, welcome the seller's relationship-building efforts, and invest their own resources to develop strong relational bonds.

Despite their logical relation, the effects of relationship investment and benefits differ. Sellers' relationship investments may generate customer relationship benefits, but they also might not, and thus, this feature has the least impact on customer commitment. The seller might strengthen the overall relationship through investments (possibly by generating feelings of gratitude), but its relative impact on customer commitment or desire to maintain a relationship is limited. In contrast, customer relationship benefits have substantial impact on customer commitment, especially compared with trust. The discrepancy in the effects on commitment may reflect the importance of actual value received by the customer. Although relationship investments that fail to generate customer value might strengthen relationships by generating debts of reciprocity (De Wulf, Odekerken-Schröder, and Iacobucci 2001, p. 34), they likely cannot generate an enduring desire to maintain a valued relationship (commitment). For example, if a seller offers tickets to Sunday's game but the customer will be out of town, the RM investment likely generates gratitude, which may improve the relationship, but not any tangible customer benefits.

Extending this example, if both the seller and the customer follow the same football team, they may enjoy *similarity*, which pertains on the individual level to commonalities in appearance, lifestyle, and status and on the organizational level to coordinating cultures, values, and goals (Nicholson, Compeau, and Sethi 2001). Similarity can indicate that the exchange partner will help facilitate goal achievement, which should strengthen the exchange relationship (Johnson and Johnson 1972), because uncertainty about the partner's actions declines when similar partners share common perspectives. The confidence inspired by similarity at both interpersonal and interorganizational levels positively affects trust, commitment, and relationship quality (Boles, Johnson, and Barksdale 2000; Doney and Cannon 1997; Nicholson, Compeau, and Sethi 2001). In turn, its strong effects on relational assets suggest some commonality may be necessary for relationship development; without common reference points, the relationship exchange likely remains purely economic or transactional rather than extending to a relational basis.

The last three antecedents studied in the meta-analysis—dependence on seller, interaction frequency, and relationship duration—have notably smaller effects, which suggests that common strategies that attempt to lock in customers, increase switching costs, or increase customer dependence may not be effective RM strategies and, in some situations, may even harm customer relationships. Dependence has the greatest positive effect on commitment, because customers prefer to maintain relationships with sellers on which they depend, but what actual customer attitudes or actions does such dependence generate? Its significantly different influence on various relationship dimensions (commitment, trust) may provide some insight. For example, increasing customer dependence can increase commitment but has a limited effect on trust, because customers grow concerned that the seller will take advantage of their dependence.

Both *relationship duration*, the length of the relationship between exchange partners, and *interaction frequency*, the number of interactions per unit of time between exchange partners, offer behavioral information in more varied situations. They therefore initiate better predictions regarding confidence or trust in the exchange partner's reliability and integrity. However, neither factor represents a good indicator of customer relationships in the meta-analysis; they both offer low correlations and negative signs at the lower bounds of the range. Even the demonstrated correlations between relationship duration and relational assets may only result from survival bias. However, the influence of interaction frequency on trust is relatively higher than that on other measures, which may imply that frequent interactions give customers more information, reduce uncertainty about future behaviors, and improve trust, even if they have no effects on the customer's satisfaction with or desire to maintain the relationship. In an exchange with high commitment but low trust (e.g., new salesperson, after a trust-destroying event), an effective RM strategy might increase the frequency of sales calls, personalized follow-ups, or customized mailings.

Overall, these findings demonstrate that different RM strategies entail widely varying levels of effectiveness. In general, the most effective strategies seem to minimize conflict; improve seller expertise, bilateral communication, relationship investments, and relationship benefits; and match both boundary spanner and organizational-level characteristics to those of targeted customers. However, increasing customer dependence and interaction frequency or just maintaining a customer relationship over time offer only minimally effective RM strategies.

Drivers of Relational Velocity Because a meta-analysis can only synthesize constructs included in many previous empirical studies, this section describes some emerging research that identifies drivers of relational growth. More specifically, based on the results from 433 relational dyads in their first six years of life, researchers have investigated the antecedents of both the level and the growth (velocity and acceleration) of commitment and trust (Palmatier et al. 2007a).

Level of conflict negatively affects the initial level of both commitment and trust and positively affects trust velocity. The strong effect of early relationship conflict on trust velocity may reflect the premise that it is easier to grow from a low level of trust; assuming the relationship endures, resolving early conflict actually builds confidence and trust in the exchange partner (Lewicki, Tomlinson, and Gillespie 2006). Similar to the results from cross-sectional research summarized in the meta-analysis, conflict has a strong negative effect on the level of relational assets (commitment and trust).

Seller expertise positively affects the initial level and negatively affects the velocity of trust; therefore, demonstrating expertise early in a relationship results in higher initial levels of trust, but those benefits are accompanied by slower subsequent growth in trust.

The results pertaining to a high level of communication in the beginning of the relationship appear quite interesting. Communication positively affects both the initial level and the velocity of trust. Thus, the initial benefit gained from communicating gets supplemented by faster growth of trust over the life of the relationship. Early communications thus appear to not only build initial trust but also help develop processes and norms that support lasting improvements in relationship interactions. This finding is consistent with expectations derived from Mohr, Fisher, and Nevin (1996) and Morgan and Hunt (1994), namely, that effective communication enables the resolution of disagreements and the alignment of goals and perspectives over the life of the relationship.

Early communications build trust and help develop processes and norms that support lasting improvements in relationship interactions.

Seller relationship investments positively affect both the initial level and the acceleration of commitment, suggesting that seller investments increase the customer's level of commitment in the first year and extend relationship length. Seller relationship investments negatively affect the velocity of commitment; thus, customers may have higher initial levels of commitment when sellers make investments early in the relationships. However, commitment is more difficult to grow from these initially higher levels, which suppresses commitment velocity. Seller relationship investments negatively affect the velocity of trust but not the initial level of trust. Research on trust also suggests that affective or relational trust (distrust) grows primarily through positive (negative) experiences (Lewicki, Tomlinson, and Gillespie 2006); thus, perhaps customers interpret heavy relationship investments by a seller as attempts to "lock them in," create unwanted debts of reciprocity, or simply make superficial advances at an early stage of the relationship (Lewicki, McAllister, and Bies 1998).

Overall, these findings suggest that several antecedents help initial levels of trust and commitment but harm future growth rates (or vice versa); communication appears to be the most universally positive antecedent in terms of strengthening initial levels of trust and commitment, as well as relating to positive growth rates in the future. Thus, early communication sets a cooperative tone for a relationship while also providing mechanisms for aligning goals and perspectives and resolving conflict. Communication is not a secret relationship marketing weapon by any means, but evidence suggests that its power remains underappreciated. Boundary spanners should be trained and motivated to engage customers in meaningful communications, especially early in the relationship.

Drivers of Relationship Breadth and Composition The minimal empirical research into the antecedents of relationship breath and composition suggests an important and underresearched distinction. To expand the breadth or density of relational contacts, group social events, training seminars, and telemarketing or direct mail may be best, because they can generate new customer prospects. But to influence relationship composition, firms may need alternative marketing strategies, such as sending senior executives or functional experts to penetrate new levels and areas within the customer firm. Although new product launches may help sellers find and access relationship contacts, they likely cannot improve the quality of the relationship alone.

Relationship Marketing Programs

Research supports the premise that different types of RM programs build different types of relational ties that generate varying levels of return (Berry 1995; Bolton, Smith, and Wagner 2003; Cannon, Achrol, and Gundlach 2000; Palmatier, Gopalakrishna, and Houston 2006; Palmatier et al. 2007c). Thus, a key question emerges: What are the relevant categories of RM programs?

Relationship Marketing Topology To describe and disaggregate RM programs, extant literature uses several criteria, including the customer bonds formed (Berry 1995), exchange control mechanisms utilized (Cannon, Achrol, and Gundlach 2000), benefits offered (Gwinner, Gremler, and Bitner 1998), functions served (Håkansson and Snehota 2000), and "content area" supported (Morgan 2000). The diverse typologies summarized in Table A3 (see Appendix) use different perspectives and criteria to identify the salient categories of relationship-building programs, but the categorization outcomes consistently include financial/economic, social, and structural components. Thus, customer–seller linkages appear similar within each category but vary in their effectiveness across categories. In this sense, a parsimonious grouping emerges under the headings of social, structural, and financial relationship marketing programs.

Social RM programs use social engagements (e.g., meals, sporting events) or frequent, customized communication to personalize the customer relationship and convey the buyer's special status. The bonds that result from such special treatment are difficult to duplicate and may prompt customers to reciprocate in the form of repeat sales and recommendations or by ignoring competitive offers (Blau 1964; De Wulf, Odekerken-Schröder, and Iacobucci 2001). Thus, social RM programs influence customer–seller relationships (Bolton, Smith, and Wagner 2003; Hennig-Thurau, Gwinner, and Gremler 2002).

By providing investments that customers likely would not make themselves, *structural RM programs*, such as an electronic order-processing interface or customized packaging, increase customer efficiency and/or productivity, resulting in a hard-to-quantify but significant customer benefit. Because such programs typically require considerable setup and offer unique benefits, their existence binds customers and sellers and likely discourages customers from switching or fragmenting their business. Strong competitive advantages also may result from structural bonds, because customers increase their business with the seller to take full advantage of these value-enhancing linkages (Berry 1995).

Finally, *financial RM programs* provide economic benefits, such as special discounts, giveaways, free shipping, or extended payment terms, in exchange for customer loyalty. However, the advantages of financial RM programs tend to be unsustainable, unless enabled by unique sources (e.g., low cost structure), because competitors easily match the programs (Day and Wensley 1988). Although customers attracted by incentives tend to be prone to deals and less profitable to serve (Cao and Gruca 2005), Bolton, Kannan, and Bramlett (2000) still find that financial programs provide sufficient returns in some situations, and Verhoef (2003) shows that loyalty programs with economic incentives enhance both customer retention and share growth. A key question still remains: Do these financial programs positively impact performance by building stronger relationships or do they function primarily as pricing incentives?

Financial Impact of Different Programs[5] In evaluating the short-term financial returns of different RM programs, Palmatier, Gopalakrishna, and Houston (2006) find that social RM investments have a direct and significant (approximately 180%) impact on profit—much greater than the impact of other types of RM investments (financial, structural). Yet social programs may cause customers to think highly of the salesperson rather than the selling firm, which increases the risk that the selling firm loses the customer if the salesperson leaves (Bendapudi and Leone 2002). Therefore, the selling firm should keep other avenues open for direct communication with customers. Despite this cautionary note, social programs can create feelings of interpersonal debt, inciting a pressing need to reciprocate and thereby generating immediate returns (Cialdini 2001). Finally, perhaps because of the interpersonal nature of their delivery (i.e., salespeople allocate resources in real time), a social program's effects appear almost immune to contextual factors.

Although structural RM investments influence profit too, they do so in a slightly different manner that depends on interaction frequency. For customers with an average interaction frequency (a few times per week), short-term returns break even (Palmatier, Gopalakrishna, and Houston 2006), but for those customers who receive frequent interactions, the return on structural RM investment is about 120%. Thus, to leverage their structural relationship marketing dollars, sellers should target customers for whom customized structural solutions offer the most value with relatively more frequent interactions. Even if customer response in the short term only breaks even, structural linkages should improve profits in the long term because customers likely want to take advantage of the value provided by structural interfaces.

Financial RM investments differ from the two previous programs (Palmatier, Gopalakrishna, and Houston 2006), largely because their ROI depends on the specific situation, yet financial RM investments fail to generate positive economic returns in any context. The absence of positive economic returns should come as no surprise; such investments often go to customers who are browsing among sellers to find the best deal. As Berry (1995, p. 240) suggests, financial RM programs "may well flunk the profitability test" because competitors can match incentives easily, and customers focused on financial incentives tend to be seriously prone to deals.

However, financial relationship marketing may have several important strategic roles. First, such investments represent a necessary response to competitive threats that helps protect existing business. Rather than going after new business, a firm that expends financial relationship marketing dollars may be on the defensive; in contrast, social and structural relationship marketing dollars represent offensive weapons. Second, to manage customer portfolios, firms must continually attract and build relationships with less valuable customers, in the hope they will grow in the long run (Johnson and Selnes 2004). In this role, financial RM as a means for long-term relationship building remains an open empirical question worthy of further investigation, but many factors clearly moderate its effectiveness. Again, this finding may indicate the relative ease with which firms appear to misallocate financial relationship marketing. A customer service employee can simply give a financial incentive (e.g., free sample, special discount); building an interpersonal relationship or implementing a structural program requires much more time and effort. Third, CRM's advantages may stem not from its ability to influence profit directly but rather from its ability to improve the allocation and targeting of marketing efforts (Mithas, Krishnan, and Fornell 2005).

RM Programs and Multilevel Relational Ties The various programs also differ in terms of their efficacy for building relationships with the seller's boundary spanner rather than the selling firm. Some programs seem naturally able to build relationships at specific levels, but this propensity can depend on factors that influence perceptions of the control over RM program allocation—that is, whether the salesperson or the selling firm maintains control. A seller's RM may positively affect financial outcomes by building customer relationship quality with *both* the selling firm and the salesperson (Palmatier et al. 2007c; Palmatier, Scheer, and Steenkamp 2007).

Although social RM programs have no distinguishable direct effect on the customer–selling firm relationship, they improve relationship quality with the salesperson, regardless of the customer's perception of control (Palmatier et al. 2007c). The salesperson's pervasive, personal role in delivering social RM benefits may create reciprocity debts, which indirectly improve relationship quality with the selling firm and lead to favorable seller financial outcomes.

Social RM programs are best for building relationship quality and generating short-term financial returns, but the relationship is typically "owned" by the boundary-spanning personnel.

In support of the conventional wisdom that structural RM builds linkages with the selling firm (Palmatier et al. 2007c), this category does not influence relationship quality with salespeople. Instead, it is purely and unambiguously beneficial for the selling firm: it provides a more sustainable competitive advantage by improving the customer's relationship with the selling firm but does not undermine the relationship with the salesperson. By default, customers associate structural RM with selling firm control, and the seller should take steps to reinforce that impression because, if the customer instead perceives salesperson control, the positive impact of structural RM on the customer–selling firm relationship can disappear.

Financial RM is more complex, largely because of the features that make it easy to copy and cause it to attract customers less likely to remain loyal. Higher perceived control by the seller improves the direct effect of financial RM on relationship quality with the selling firm, but at the interpersonal level, even this favorable impact gets undermined by the parallel negative effect because if the customer does not perceive the salesperson as an advocate, the customer–salesperson relationship suffers.

In summary, to build relationship quality and generate short-term financial returns, firms should choose social programs but must recognize the dangers of relying solely on relational ties with the seller's boundary-spanning personnel. If an employee "owns" the customer relationship, the relationship provides value only as long as the employee stays with the firm; if the employee leaves, the relationship is lost or, worse yet, becomes profitable for the employee's new firm. According to a longitudinal analysis, salesperson-owned loyalty drives sales growth, but such growth disappears when salespeople move to competitors (Palmatier, Scheer, and Steenkamp 2007).

Structural RM programs appear to pay dividends to sellers, but possibly over a longer time, and they may perform better with more active customers. Because structural programs appear to operate at the firm level, they are not as susceptible to specific employee actions—unless the employee convinces the customer that he or she controlled allocations, in which case the seller loses most of the beneficial aspects of the program.

Most interesting of all, financial RM programs do not appear to generate either relationship quality or short-term financial returns; in some cases, they even damage the relationship. For example, when customers perceive that salespeople control the financial program, they pull away from relationships with the selling firm; if they perceive the firm as the controlling party, they evince little interest in a relationship with the salesperson (Palmatier et al. 2007c). Thus, financial RM programs probably should be used only as a defense strategy, not an offensive relationship-building strategy.

Yet the poor performance of financial RM programs may seem surprising, considering they are the most common type of program that top retail, travel, financial services, and consumer product companies employ. Many programs use a points system to provide discounts or rewards to high-volume customers, especially in B2C contexts, though most academic RM research investigates the B2B context. Recent trends are shifting customer interfaces away from direct-selling organizations and local call centers to automated and remote call systems, which reduces the level of social RM even further. Firms may be beginning to understand the poor returns generated from many financial programs; as the popular press reports (Trachtenberg 2007, p. D1), "Borders [Books] slashes buyer rewards, cuts discounts," even though the program was a "tremendous hit with consumers." Many companies (e.g., Best Buy, Staples, MCI, Hertz, Citibank, United Airlines) similarly are reducing the costs of their financially focused RM programs.

Financial RM programs do not appear to generate either relationship quality or short-term financial returns; in some cases, they actually damage the relationship.

Organizational Elements and Business Processes

Even though firms often spend most of their time and RM investment dollars on implementing, managing, and funding specific RM programs, various aspects of the firm's business have a strong effect on customer–seller relationships. For example, the top three effects on customer relationships are conflict, seller expertise, and communication (Table 3, p. 57), whereas relationship investments and benefits generated from RM programs rank fourth and sixth, respectively (Palmatier et al. 2006). Thus, if RM programs, as represented by relationship investments and benefits, are not the most critical factors, and other factors are also important, how do a firm's organizational elements and business processes influence the firm's customer relationships and relational assets?

According to organizational design theory (Tushman and Nadler 1978), five elements and their related business processes constitute the most relevant dimensions of an organization: strategy, leadership, culture, structure, and control. As separate but interrelated components, and in addition to specific RM programs, the five elements determine the effectiveness of a firm's RM efforts. In one study, Reichheld (2001, p. 83) shows that *employees'* reactions to the statement, "I believe this organization deserves my loyalty" is one of the best predictors of *customer* loyalty, reinforcing the critical role of organizational elements in determining how a firm deals with its customers.

The impact of the organization's *strategy* on its ability to build and maintain strong customer relationships pervades the other organizational elements, which are guided and driven by the firm's strategy. For example, in the retail context, Wal-Mart has chosen to be an everyday-low-price supplier, whereas Nordstrom aims to be a premium niche supplier; in both cases, strategy cascades throughout the firm by influencing the culture (cost versus customer centric), leadership (centralized versus distributive), structure (focus on store versus focus on boundary spanner through selection and training), and control (hourly salary with detailed rules versus commission with general guidelines), which means it ultimately affects the firm's ability to build and maintain customer relationships. Wal-Mart's low-cost strategy interrelates with other organizational elements, such that Wal-Mart has a harder time building strong customer–seller relationships than does Nordstrom.

The firm's *leadership* can catalyze organizational effectiveness, because the upper echelon's beliefs shape the course of their organization, and their expertise drives strategy and performance (Weinzimmer et al. 2003). Thus, when those belief structures align with the RM paradigm, the firm's relationship-building efforts should benefit; as Jaworski and Kohli (1993) argue, employees in market-oriented firms receive clear messages from top management about the importance of customers.

In a firm context, *culture* refers to the "system of shared values and norms that define appropriate attitudes and behaviors for organizational members" (O'Reilly and Chatman 1996, p. 166); in turn, shared norms about customers should help determine a firm's relational assets. To exploit customer relationships as a sustainable competitive advantage, "[a] relationship orientation must pervade the mind-set, values, and norms of the organization" (Day 2000, p. 24), and a market-oriented culture can prompt relational behaviors and ultimately enhance financial performance (Cannon and Perreault 1999, p. 456). A "pro-customer" culture or climate thus appears necessary to generate superior returns from customer–seller relationships or ensure the success of CRM initiatives (Homburg and Pflesser 2000). Culture—those values, norms, and artifacts prevalent in an organization—thus may amplify or attenuate customer relationship initiatives.

Organizational *structure* captures how employees are organized and customer interface activities are arranged to support new and existing customer relationships. Organizational structures are created around three types of processes with the potential to affect customer relationships. Outside-in processes (e.g., market sensing, customer linking, channel bonding, technology monitoring), inside-out processes (e.g., costs, logistics, human resources), and spanning processes (e.g., order fulfillment, customer service, delivery) all bridge the front and back ends of an organization (Day 1994). Therefore, decisions about organizational structure and processes affect service quality, service failure resolution, the competence of boundary spanners, the ability and level of communication, and the number and ability of contact points, all of which in turn affect customer–seller relationships. Firms often make organizational structural decisions based on cost or internal considerations, without fully understanding the implications for their customer relationships. For example, moving customer call centers offshore provides significant cost savings but also can seriously degrade customer relationships (e.g., Dell's well-documented experience). Three of the top five drivers of strong customer relationships—boundary spanner's expertise, similarity to the customer, and ability to communicate effectively—are particularly harmed by such a change (Palmatier et al. 2006).

However, different industries require different amounts of customer contact (e.g., services versus manufacturing). Firms in high-contact industries should empower boundary spanners, who are close to customers, whereas low-contact companies should empower the production staff, who are close to necessary resources (Chase and Tansik 1983). When firms provide both products and services, they face a difficult choice: develop two separate organizations and lose the benefits of product–service synergies, or use a single structure that does not align optimally with either products or services.

Finally, the system designed to monitor, incentivize, or punish employees according to their customer interface activities entails the *control* element (Oliver and Anderson 1994). If sellers want their employees to focus on building relationships, not just closing the sale, they should adopt reward systems that measure relationship quality. (Weitz and Bradford 1999); standards, metrics, and feedback loops similarly help optimize performance and learning for CRM initiatives (Payne and Frow 2005).

In summary, the five elements of organizational design and their associated business processes, along with RM programs, influence a firm's ability to build and maintain strong customer–seller relationships and should be considered in aggregate. In some cases, poor returns on RM programs may be due to the lack of alignment or consistency among the program and the organization's overall strategy, leadership direction, organizational structure, cultural norms, or control mechanisms. More research should attempt to isolate the relative effects of diverse drivers of relational assets to determine if RM programs depend on specific organizational elements.

6

Targeting and Adapting Relationship Marketing Strategies

The previous discussion focused on the causal linkages responsible for the effectiveness of relationship marketing (RM activities → relational assets → relational behaviors → financial outcomes) (as outlined in Figure 6, p. 44), but in most cases, the discussion ignores how these linkages vary depending on specific contextual factors. For example, seller expertise, on average, represents the most significant positive antecedent to relational assets (i.e., average results across all customers in the meta-analysis), but its influence might depend on specific customer factors: customers rebuying a commodity product (e.g., gasoline) have little interest in expertise, whereas customers buying a highly technical product (e.g., HDTV) find significant value in such an RM activity.

The next four sections detail how the linkages in the RM causal chain vary according to customer, seller, multilevel relationship, and environmental factors. Understanding the contingencies of RM strategies should enable managers to target customers with specific RM activities or adapt strategies to optimize returns on their marketing investments.

Customer Factors[6]

Because RM is not effective for all customers (Cao and Gruca 2005; Reichheld and Teal 1996; Reinartz and Kumar 2000) and some customers seek to avoid relationships (Berry 1995; Crosby, Evans, and Cowles 1990), sellers must determine where to allocate RM resources across their customer portfolios. Common sense would suggest that customers that are receptive to relationship building are the best candidates for strong relationships, and research supports this assumption (Anderson and Narus 1991; Dwyer, Schurr, and Oh 1987). More particularly, RM succeeds among customers that require a relational governance structure to solve their specific governance problems (e.g., uncertainty, dependence), whose potential problems cannot be fully predicted or addressed in advance, and that lack other governance protections (Heide 1994; Pfeffer and Salancik 1978; Williamson 1985).

Customer Relationship Orientation The factors that increase a customer's desire to engage in a strong relationship with a partner, or *relationship orientation* (RO), also should increase receptivity to relationship building and result in more effective RM. Customers with a high RO likely reciprocate the seller's RM efforts by, for example, responding positively to a seller's request for a meeting or information. If both exchange partners prefer a strong relationship, they have aligned goals, are more motivated to communicate freely and disclose intimate information, and probably will not initiate conflict. Such goal similarity, two-way communication, and minimal conflict build strong relationships with customers that desire them.

Relationship marketing to customers with a low RO generates costs beyond what the company wants to incur. Relationship marketing imposes costs on the customer; the customer incurs at least the opportunity costs associated with communicating with the seller and receiving and using RM programs. Thus, for customers with a low RO, the exchange appears inefficient because the customer perceives little need for relational governance or relationship building. Imagine a customer who contacts a seller's central call center to obtain a product sample but then must endure an extended follow-up visit full of queries, small talk, and relationship-building entreaties from the salesperson who delivers the sample. Whereas this customer perceives no need for a relationally based exchange to acquire the sample and thus assesses the exchange as inefficient, another customer with a high RO would likely consider the same efforts beneficial and an efficient use of time because those efforts help build the desired governance structure.

As another form of cost, RM creates interpersonal reciprocity obligations, which can cause consumers personal discomfort until they are repaid and thus entail additional consumer costs. Consumers with a low RO may purposefully avoid sellers that shower them with unwanted benefits; because not reciprocating may make the consumer appear impolite and suffer a sense of guilt (Cialdini 2001). By repaying a reciprocity obligation, consumers with a high RO can deepen their relationship with the seller, perhaps even overcompensating repayment. Paradoxically, the same underlying psychological processes and reciprocity norms can both enhance relationship building with relationally oriented consumers and drive away those with a low RO.

Even when RM activities do not impose direct costs on the customer, the customer likely recognizes the seller's costs for engaging in these activities, which could be reflected in higher sales prices. Frequent mailings or calls impose few direct costs on the customer, but a customer with a low RO may evaluate a seller that wastes resources on such efforts unfavorably.

> *The same psychological processes and reciprocity norms can enhance relationship building with relationally oriented consumers and drive away those with a low relationship orientation.*

To optimize RM effectiveness, sellers must match the level of RM activities to the customer's RO. Without knowledge about that level, the firm risks either an insufficient investment in RM programs or an exaggerated investment that wastes precious marketing resources and generates unwanted customer costs. This latter effect also incites customer perceptions of exchange inefficiency that degrade relational assets and seller performance (Palmatier et al. 2008). Overall, customer RO leverages RM activities and thus can result in stronger relationships and improved financial performance.

The factors that may promote a customer's desire for relational governance consist of various stable and exchange-specific aspects. Stable factors include those elements, at any level, that remain constant across all exchanges, such as industry norms (Heide and John 1992) or the customer's intrinsic characteristics (Christy, Oliver, and Penn 1996; Schutz 1992). Exchange-specific factors pertain to elements that vary across different exchange contexts, such as exchange partner characteristics (Bendapudi and Berry 1997) or product-based details (De Wulf, Odekerken-Schröder, and Iacobucci 2001). Table A4 summarizes research into the drivers of customer RO (see Appendix).

Stable factors promoting customer relationship orientation At the environmental, industry, organizational, and individual levels, several factors remain constant across customer–seller interactions. *Industry relational norms* vary across industries but reflect the stable value placed on customer–supplier relationships within an industry (Heide and John 1992; Macaulay 1963), such that each industry has an "industry bandwidth of working relationships" that "reflects the explicit or implicit relationship strategies" (Anderson and Narus 1991, p. 96). In turn, each industry's typical relational practices affect customers' receptivity to relationship-building efforts and customer RO (Palmatier et al. 2008).

Also at the industry level, *industry uncertainty* captures volatility, the difficulty of monitoring industry changes, and the rapidity of technological changes (Celly and Frazier 1996). According to transaction cost economics, greater exchange uncertainty increases the need for adaptability, which stems from relational bonds between exchange partners (Noordewier, John, and Nevin 1990;

Williamson 1985). Thus, stronger relationships with exchange partners enhance adaptations to expected but unpredictable changes (Cannon and Perreault 1999; Noordewier, John, and Nevin 1990).

At the firm level, *relation-centric reward systems* encourage strong customer–supplier relationships through evaluation systems, compensation programs, and policies. If a (customer) employee's rewards depend mostly on price reductions, multiple sourcing, or the number of transactions, the employee will embrace a transaction orientation, but if an employee receives relationship-building incentives, he or she should exhibit a relational orientation.

Finally, *relationship proneness* refers to the basic tendency to engage in relationships (De Wulf, Odekerken-Schröder, and Iacobucci 2001). Consistent with Schutz's (1992) research on interpersonal relationship proneness across different settings, relationship proneness is a stable, individual difference variable, such that a relationally prone customer experiences a higher RO toward sellers (Johnson 1999; Johnson and Sohi 2001).

Exchange-specific factors promoting customer relationship orientation Elements unique to the particular exchange context, such as selling firm characteristics, salesperson characteristics, and unique product features, also may promote an RO among customers (see Figure 7). For example, a highly *competent salesperson* who is capable across a range of relevant tasks (Doney and Cannon 1997) can solve problems, reduce the exchange's transaction costs, and ensure more successful exchanges; people prefer a strong relationship with a competent partner (Crosby, Evans, and Cowles 1990).

Resource dependence theory suggests relationship building enables a party to manage (Pfeffer and Salancik 1978) or counteract its dependence (Ganesan 1994; Heide and John 1988) on exchange partners. A customer's *product dependence*, or need to develop a relationship to acquire specific products with the greatest efficiency, promotes a higher RO.

Higher customer involvement causes more customers to desire a relationship (De Wulf, Odekerken-Schröder, and Iacobucci 2001) and perceive opportunities for generating value from relationships. In this sense, *product category involvement* reflects the importance a customer places on a product category, which may stem from personal-, firm-, or role-related needs, values, and interests (Mittal 1995), and in turn increases a customer's RO.

Importance of aligning RM with customer relationship orientation As much research indicates, RM can be costly and even undermine relationships in certain cases (Cao and Gruca 2005; Colgate and Danaher 2000; Dowling and Uncles 1997), which also means that alignment with customers' relationship needs likely drives seller performance more than does the pursuit of ever closer

Figure 7
Role of Customer Relationship Orientation in Relationship Marketing Effectiveness

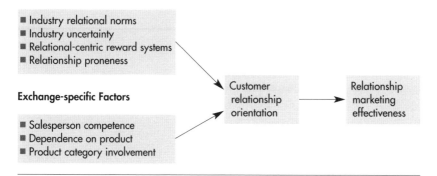

Stable Factors

- Industry relational norms
- Industry uncertainty
- Relational-centric reward systems
- Relationship proneness

Exchange-specific Factors

- Salesperson competence
- Dependence on product
- Product category involvement

Customer relationship orientation → Relationship marketing effectiveness

customer–seller relationships. As Cannon and Perreault (1999, p. 456) observe post hoc, "If relationships meet customer needs, they are likely to endure, no matter how closely connected," but "closer relationships do not necessarily mean higher performance" (p. 454). And as Noordewier, John, and Nevin (1990, p. 91) report, "[B]uying firms can realize enhanced performance by crafting an 'appropriate' governance structure"; similarly, Reinartz and Kumar (2000) acknowledge that transactional customers may be as profitable as long-term, relational customers. Matching RM efforts to the customer's relationship governance requirements (relationship orientation) balances the flexibility, monitoring, and safeguarding benefits received by customers in relationally based exchanges with the added costs the customer incurs in building and maintaining those relationships.

For customers with a higher RO, RM enhances relationship quality and leads them to perceive exchange efficiency, which improves relational assets and, ultimately, seller performance (Palmatier et al. 2008). In this way, RO offers key information about a party's receptivity to RM efforts and need—or lack of need—for a relational governance structure.

Understanding a customer's RO becomes even more crucial in the face of modern cost-reducing and productivity-enhancing efforts that minimize business customers' time to meet with sellers, as well as sellers' increased relationship-building efforts. According to one study, customers with a low RO would shift 21% of their business to another supplier if it offered completely automated transactions (i.e., no salesperson) (Palmatier et al. 2008). Because past patronage cannot predict the future behavior of low RO customers, sellers could save substantial expenses, improve service to existing customers, and lure away competitors' customers if they were able to detect low RO customers accurately and offer them arm's-length interactions (e.g., electronic interface). Thus, firms should segment customers based on their relationship orientation and use this information to better target RM investments. Table A5 summarizes the items used to measure customer relationship orientation (see Appendix).

Organizational policies or procedures that promote relationship building, such as training or compensation systems that indiscriminately motivate salespeople to engage in intensive relationship building, may alienate many customers, especially those with a low RO. But if the vast majority of a firm's customer base exhibits a high RO, a corporate relationship orientation (Day 2000) may generate sustainable competitive advantage. Finally, a portfolio of customers distributed evenly across the RO spectrum demands a balanced approach, because a unilateral corporate emphasis on building customer relationships creates unnecessary expenses and misalignments with the relational governance preferences of many customers.

Turnover and Difficulty of Accessing Customer Boundary Spanners In addition to the factors that may increase a customer's RO (desire for a relationship), do other customer factors, which do not affect desire for a relationship, still make RM strategies more effective? When network researchers apply contingency theory, which argues that the effectiveness of firm actions depends on fit with structural and contextual factors (Donaldson 2001; Drazin and Van de Ven 1985), they discover that the impact of network characteristics on performance also depends on contextual factors (Mohrman, Tenkasi, and Mohrman 2003; Stevenson and Greenberg 2000). Similarly, contingency theory suggests that interfirm relationship drivers (quality, breath, and composition) generate more value in certain situations.

For example, providing access to information sources and sales opportunities and mitigating the negative effect of the turnover of contact personnel through diverse customer-contact points, relationship breadth, or density can enhance a seller's profits. Just as a team selling approach may reduce the negative effect of salesperson turnover (Bendapudi and Leone 2002), a seller with more interfirm ties (relationship breadth) can replace any specific relational tie more easily by shifting the transaction to another tie or quickly rebuilding a bond with a new contact (perhaps through group diffusion from other relational contacts; Brown 2000). Relationship breadth has a greater performance impact when contact turnover is high (Palmatier 2008; Palmatier 2007). Sales managers dealing with companies that experience high employee turnover therefore should aggressively expand the breadth of their contact portfolio to build a customer team.

The number of relational ties has a greater impact on performance in situations characterized by high levels of customer contact turnover.

Because it increases the seller's access to valuable, nonredundant information and ability to identify and overcome selling barriers, relationship composition can enhance sales and profits. If the customer decision makers are easy to approach, competitors can access the same information, respond quickly, and build their own relational ties, which undermine some seller benefits. But if the seller knows and can access key decision makers whom other sellers have trouble accessing, it gains better information, reduces competition, and achieves a greater ability to overcome selling barriers. Therefore, as the difficulty of interfacing with the customer increases, relationship composition's impact on the seller's ability to generate profits also increases (Palmatier 2007). In an interesting conundrum, those customers that are the most difficult to access and deal with may be the most valuable, and those that are easy to access may generate lower returns, all else being equal. Thus, even if salespeople prefer visiting customers that are receptive to meeting, they might enhance their performance if they were to shift resources to firms or contacts that are more difficult to access.

Factors Leveraging Effect of Customer Gratitude on Behavior Feelings of gratitude affect short-term customer behavior in response to RM activities (Morales 2005; Palmatier et al. 2007b), but which factors can enhance a customer's emotional gratitude? Existing literature reveals several elements, including perceptions about the amount of free will that the seller has, the motives the seller has, and the amount of risk the seller takes in making that investment.

When people do something of their own accord, they are acting of their own free will. Examples of free will (versus contractual behavior) include giving an unexpected gift or performing a random act of kindness. Therefore, an investment takes on additional meaning if it is not part of a contract or formal RM program. For example, if an employee expects to receive a salary increase next year, as specified by his or her labor contract, that employee probably does not feel grateful to his or her boss for the increase. But if the boss offers a raise because the employee is doing a great job, that employee likely feels more appreciation because the boss is not obligated to give it. Recipients of such meaningful investments tend to feel gratitude; in contrast, contractual, role-based, or persuasion-based investments decrease feelings of gratitude (Morales 2005; Tsang 2006). People feel most grateful to benefactors when they perceive that the positive behaviors are under the benefactors' volitional control (Weiner 1985). Thus, higher levels of gratitude result from RM investments when the customer perceives those investments as an act of free will rather than a con-tractual fulfillment, program requirement, or duty-based obligation (Emmons and McCullough 2004; Gouldner 1960; Palmatier et al. 2007b).

A *motive* represents a desire or need that incites action, and people often ponder others' motives. Customer inferences about motives play key roles in their perceptions of sellers' actions, such that they tend to experience gratitude when the favor is perceived to communicate benevolent intentions rather than an underlying ulterior motive. Tesser, Gatewood, and Driver (1968) demonstrate in laboratory scenarios that perceptions of benevolent versus self-serving motives significantly affect the amount of gratitude felt by the recipient of a favor or gift, and Tsang (2006) demonstrates that gratitude levels for favors given with ulterior motives are half those for favors with benevolent motives. Thus, the customer's view of the seller's motive for an investment affects the gratitude he or she feels and future behavior.

Relationship building often begins with an investment (e.g., time, effort), and in a noncontractual context, the person who initiates the investment gen-erally does so at a cost. Along with this cost, the person experiences the risk, defined as the subjective possibility that the investment may not lead to recip-rocated behavior. Typically, buyer–seller relational exchanges begin with an investment that is costly to the seller, and because of the risk of that investment, the customer tends to feel gratitude in response to the benefit received (Tesser, Gatewood, and Driver 1968; Tsang 2006). Appreciating something (e.g., event, person, behavior, object) involves noticing and acknowledging its value or meaning and feeling a positive emotional connection to it (Adler and Fagley 2005). Most people appreciate a gift, especially when that gift contains value, and value and appreciation increase when the gift represents a needed item. Need refers to the condition in which a person requires or desires something, such that when a need exists (versus no need), the pertinent item or situation entails higher value. When a recipient obtains an item with such value, his or her gratitude increases (Tesser, Gatewood, and Driver 1968; Tsang 2006).

Customer gratitude and, hence, RM effectiveness are enhanced as perceptions of the seller's free will, benevolent motives, and risk in making the investment increase.

Seller Factors

Characteristics of the seller side of the exchange dyad may alter RM effectiveness. For example, customer relational assets have greater impacts for firms that sell services versus products, deal with channel partners rather than direct customers, and sell to business customers versus consumers (Palmatier et al. 2006).

Because services are less tangible, less consistent, and more perishable than products, and demand customer and boundary spanner involvement in their production and consumption (Zeithaml, Parasuraman, and Berry 1985), stronger relationships between customers and sellers appear more critical for services than for products. Furthermore, because evaluations of service offerings tend to be more ambiguous, the intangibility of services may make the benefits of trust more critical.

Exchanges between channel partners entail greater interdependence and require coordinated action to prevent opportunistic behavior and ensure success (Anderson and Weitz 1989), as compared to direct customer–seller transactions (Anderson and Weitz 1989; Kumar, Scheer, and Steenkamp 1995a). To facilitate coordinated actions and limit opportunistic behaviors, channel partners must engage in strong relationships, which have a greater impact on exchange performance than they would in simple, direct exchanges between sellers and customers.

The importance of relationships actually serves as a means to distinguish consumer and business markets; as Anderson and Narus (2004, p. 21) maintain, a "firm's success in business markets depends directly on its working relationships." Because working relationships are more critical in B2B markets, relationships have a greater impact on exchange outcomes in these contexts than in B2C markets.

The decision makers who allocate relationship marketing investments must be able and motivated to make efficient choices to increase overall RM program effectiveness. For example, *experienced salespeople* can select, align, and deliver targeted programs to certain customers (Weitz, Sujan, and Sujan 1986), which implies that RM likely affects them more in terms of performance. Such motivation may stem from ownership interest in the selling firm, which prompts salespeople to act in the best interests of the firm (Bergen, Dutta, and Walker 1992). However, without *ownership interest*, and if earnings depend on sales revenue, the goals of the salespeople and the firm may become unaligned. In this case, salespeople with discretion over their expenditures could expend resources on their own customers without worrying about direct costs or overall return on RM investments. In contrast, when they possess ownership interest, salespeople target their relationship-building resources more carefully to minimize inefficient spending (Palmatier, Gopalakrishna, and Houston 2006).

When firms employ CRM, they can generate greater profits from a given relationship-building investment (Boulding et al. 2005; Palmatier, Gopalakrishna, and Houston 2006), because dedicated CRM processes and systems motivate and enable employees to allocate marketing resources efficiently, systematically, and proactively (Mithas, Krishnan, and Fornell 2005; Reinartz, Krafft, and Hoyer 2004). The systems might identify customers that meet criteria for specific programs (Chen and Iyer 2002), evaluate and improve program effectiveness, or reduce the time needed to implement a program.

As an example, consider the hierarchical nested data collected in a study of an interfirm relationship. The research isolates the variance explained by multiple sources (customer, salesperson, and selling firm) from the impact of RM program investments on the seller's returns (Palmatier, Gopalakrishna, and Houston 2006). In this B2B context, 62% of variance in return occurs at the customer level, 10% lies at the salesperson level, and the remaining 28% appears at the firm level. That is, RM effectiveness depends on multilevel factors, but surprisingly, the salesperson level has little influence. However, post hoc explanations suggest that the salespeople in the sample are relatively homogenous in terms of experience and capabilities, so the relative importance of customer and selling firm factors increases.

Multilevel Relationship Factors

Perceived Selling Firm Consistency Customers experience relational ties with both the selling firm as a group and the seller's primary boundary spanner (e.g., salesperson), which highlights the complexity of interfirm exchanges but also suggests a potential impact of contextual factors on outcomes and the location of relationships (i.e., customer–selling firm or customer–salesperson). When the customer relationship exists with an individual rather than a group or firm, it has a greater impact on exchange outcomes (O'Laughlin and Malle 2002;

Palmatier et al. 2006; Palmatier et al. 2007c; Palmatier, Scheer, and Steenkamp 2007), because customers use recall decision heuristics to evaluate behaviorally inconsistent selling firms (Hamilton and Sherman 1996; Hilton and von Hippel 1990). However, if the firm appears to offer high *entitativity*, exhibiting characteristics of a single, coherent entity, customers' judgment-formation processes become more similar to the online models that they use to evaluate individuals (Campbell 1958; Hamilton and Sherman 1996). Therefore, judgments about highly entitative, consistent firms are stronger and more robust than those about typical, less entitative groups (Palmatier et al. 2007c; Palmatier, Scheer, and Steenkamp 2007).

In turn, *perceived selling-firm consistency* plays an important moderating role, such that the customer's increased perceptions of the selling firm as a coherent entity make the customer more likely to use an online model to form judgments, have greater confidence in those judgments, and enact behavior based on those judgments. If all selling firm employees behave consistently, the customer logically infers that their actions reflect underlying selling firm norms or characteristics, so future dealings with the firm should remain consistent, even if they involve different associates. When, for example, a customer issues a special request to sellers, perceptions of consistency become crucial; assuming similar levels of trust in all sellers, the customer likely chooses the consistent firm as a result of its stronger, more confident inferences about the likelihood that the seller can meet any promises made by any salesperson. In this scenario, the consistent selling firm achieves superior financial outcomes. The effectiveness of relationship marketing increases as the customer perceives the seller firm's employees, policies, and behaviors as more consistent and coherent.

Perceived Control of Relationship Marketing Activities Some RM activities work to build loyal relationships at the level of the salesperson (e.g., free lunch) or selling firm (e.g., corporate loyalty program), but beyond that effort, the customer's perceptions of the source of RM benefits—that is, the customer's attributions of the *perceived control* of RM benefits—can shift effects to different relationship levels (Palmatier et al. 2007c), depending on the degree to which the customer attributes the RM benefit to a specific boundary spanner or the selling firm. Yet customers are rarely aware of actual funding arrangements (e.g., behind-the-scenes incentives, cost-sharing programs), so they must rely on cues and historical observations (Menon et al. 1999) to infer the locus of control (Weiner 1986). The extent of a salesperson's allocation control often varies according to that salesperson's experience or past performance, ranging from total discretion to complete firm control. Even if the selling firm mandates certain RM benefits, salespeople may claim credit to create an interpersonal reciprocity debt (Cialdini 2001), because a salesperson valued by the customer gains greater leverage within his or her selling firm. However, attributions for a marketing program also depend on the positioning of the program. Considering the content, nature, and implementation of a program, the customer establishes a bottom-line control attribution that dictates whether relationship-building effects fall on the customer–selling firm or the customer–salesperson relationship.

In summary, the benefits of RM emerge as a result of enhanced interpersonal and person-to-firm relationships. Strong salesperson–customer relationships can benefit the seller in several ways, such as a positive spillover of relationship quality to the selling firm, higher sales levels, and enhanced financial performance. However, these enhancements dictate that the firm depends on its critical salespeople. Managers therefore must balance the potential payoffs of customer–salesperson interpersonal relationships with the risk of salesperson turnover. With consistent behavior by boundary spanners, firms can strengthen the impact of the less volatile customer–selling firm relationship, reduce the risk of loss, and better align with recent trends toward team selling and "multiple customer touch points" managed through CRM systems.

Whether an RM program builds customer relationships with the selling firm or the salesperson depends on the type of program and on the customer's perception of who provides that program.

Environmental Factors

Environmental Uncertainty The external context in which relationships are embedded also likely moderates the effects of RM on performance, especially when that context is uncertain. As environmental uncertainty increases, exchange partners need to adapt and require enhanced flexibility and behavioral confidence, which mark relational- as opposed to transactional-based exchanges (Cannon and Perreault 1999; Dahlstrom and Nygaard 1995). Therefore, higher uncertainty should enhance the positive effect of commitment, trust, interdependence, and relational norms on exchange outcomes. Similarly, relational bonds limit conflict, a capability that grows even more important in turbulent environments, with their increased likelihood of disagreement and need for negotiation to achieve solutions.

In support of the benefits of flexible, relational-based exchanges, Cannon, Achrol, and Gundlach (2000) note that relational norms enhance performance in high-uncertainty conditions. Joshi and Stump (1999) find that decision-making uncertainty positively moderates the impact of specific investments on cooperation and joint action. Integrating both relational and transaction cost perspectives, Noordewier, John, and Nevin (1990) reveal that relational governance's effect on performance depends on uncertainty. Finally, in a longitudinal analysis of interfirm relationships, Palmatier, Dant, and Grewal (2007) show that as environmental uncertainty increases, so do the positive effects of commitment, trust, and relational norms on cooperation and financial performance. That is, in uncertain environments, relational-based exchanges outperform transaction-based ones, and the greater adaptability and flexibility associated with relationally governed exchanges appear to pay greater dividends.

Customer relationships generate higher returns in conditions of environmental uncertainty.

Culture Because most RM research has been conducted in the United States and Western Europe, it is reasonable to question whether existing findings and strategies are equally effective in other cultural settings. A recent review of cross-cultural relationship marketing research (Samiee and Walters 2003, p. 206) summarizes the state of affairs: "International relationship marketing literature is relatively impoverished." This section therefore recounts the brief research that investigates the role of culture in RM (Elahee, Kirby, and Nasif 2002; Hewett, Money, and Sharma 2006; Samiee and Walters 2003).

Ndubisi (2004) offers a conceptual argument detailing how five dimensions of Hofstede's (1997) cultural topology may affect relationship marketing. First, with regard to power distance, or the acceptance among less powerful members of the culture of unequal power distributions, RM should be more effective in low power-distance cultures, such as the United States, because less stratification among members creates fewer barriers to building relationships.

Second, individualism versus collectivism captures the degree to which the society forms groups. Relationship marketing should be more effective in collectivist cultures, such as Japan, that already recognize the salience of relationships for the social structure and attempt to suppress self-interested behaviors. Hewett, Money, and Sharma (2006) similarly indicate that relationship strength has a greater impact on repurchase intentions in Latin America (collectivist culture) than in the United States (individualist culture).

Third, in masculine societies (e.g., Japan), men are more competitive, assertive, and driven by outcomes, whereas in a feminine society (e.g., the Scandinavian countries), the roles of men and women are more similar, less competitive, and more nurturing. Ndubisi (2004) argues that RM is more effective in the latter, where values are more consistent with spending time and effort to build long-term relationships and whose members are less competitive and more empathetic, which supports relational ties.

Fourth, uncertainty avoidance refers to the degree to which members are bothered by uncertain or ambiguous situations. For example, Chinese people try to minimize the chance of losing face, which increases their desire to build relational ties to decrease the uncertainty of the exchange (Ndubisi 2004). Dealing with new exchange partners is often a risky and uncertain venture, so relationship orientation should be higher in societies with higher levels of uncertainty avoidance.

Fifth and finally, a long-term orientation reflects a focus on long-term goals and more permanent outcomes. In long-term-oriented societies, such as Asia, RM should be more effective, because these cultures invest today for relational payoffs in the future. Alternatively, short-term cultures like the United States focus more on extracting the greatest benefits they can from a single transaction, which can undermine their long-term relationships.

In summary, research supports the notion that culture is an important RM factor, such that sellers in cultures that are less power distant, more collectivist, and more feminist, and have higher uncertainty avoidance and longer-term orientations should achieve higher returns on their RM investments (Elahee, Kirby, and Nasif 2002; Hewett, Money, and Sharma 2006; Samiee and Walters 2003). Additional research could isolate the relative effects of these dimensions and provide systematic RM guidance regarding the differences across major economic regions.

7

Enhancing Performance Through Best Practice

To provide concise and actionable guidance for managers involved in designing and implementing RM strategies, this section synthesizes and reorganizes the preceding material. More specifically, it uses theory and empirical research to provide insight into two crucial decisions in relationship marketing—how to build and maintain strong customer relationships, and how to adapt and target RM—to develop several generalizations. To minimize redundancy, the actual underlying research and theories are not discussed here; instead, the goal is to provide concise, actionable guidance for managers involved in RM practice. Tables 4 and 5 provide a summary of RM best practices.

How to Build and Maintain Strong Customer Relationships

The factor with the most significant impact on customer relationship quality is unresolved conflict, which can undo many years and dollars spent on relationship building. In many cases, it becomes counterproductive to increase RM budgets without a well-designed process for dealing with customer problems, service failures, or violations of trust. Thus, *sellers must address customer conflict resolution within the framework of their overall RM activities*, possibly by empowering boundary spanners to address issues themselves (e.g., Ritz Carlton employees can spend up to $1,000 solving customer issues), building a culture that emphasizes the importance of resolving conflict, and instituting formal systems for correcting customer issues.

It may be counterproductive to increase RM budgets without a well-designed process for dealing with customer problems, service failures, or violations of trust.

The individual, boundary-spanning personnel with whom customers interface often represent the most critical vehicle for building and maintaining

Table 4
Best Practices: How to Build and Maintain Strong Customer Relationships

■ Do not let conflict go unresolved, because it will overwhelm other relationship-building efforts.

■ Assign customers a dedicated contact person, even if customers interface through multiple channels (e.g., call center, online).

■ Focus the largest portion of RM investments on selecting, training, and motivating boundary-spanning employees, who represent the most effective means to build and maintain relationships.

■ Relationship marketing investments dedicated to specific programs should be primarily allocated to social and structural programs.

■ Minimize the proactive use of financial RM programs (e.g., price rebates, points programs) for relationship building; rather consider these programs as price/volume discounts or competitive responses.

■ Boundary spanners should be given allocation control of most social programs, but allocation control of structural and financial programs should not fully reside with boundary spanners.

■ If facing high turnover of boundary spanners, sellers should increase the consistency across boundary spanners, reallocate spending from social to structural programs, and reduce boundary spanners' discretionary control of RM programs.

■ Institute RM programs focused on increasing the amount, frequency, and quality of communication with customers, especially early in the relationship lifecycle, because communication is a strong driver of relationship quality and future relationship growth (relational velocity).

■ Measure multiple aspects of relational assets (relationship quality, breadth, composition, and growth/velocity) on an ongoing basis.

■ Conduct RM audits to verify seller's organizational elements (firm strategy, leadership, culture, structures, and control) and business processes are aligned with RM objectives.

Table 5
Best Practices: How to Target and Adapt Relationship Marketing

■ The effectiveness of RM can be enhanced by actively targeting investments toward customers with high relationship orientation (need and desire for a relationship).

■ Leverage RM investments by designing programs to increase customers' perceptions of seller's free will, benevolence, risk, and cost in providing the RM benefit (leave some random or discretionary element to programs).

■ Leverage RM investments by providing the benefit when the customer's need is the highest and the benefit provides the most value.

■ Give customers an opportunity to reciprocate soon after receiving a RM benefit (not quid pro quo), which takes advantage of high levels of gratitude, prevents guilt rationalization, and leads to the formation of reciprocity norms.

■ In interfirm relationships, target RM programs toward specific relationship weaknesses (i.e., relationship quality, breadth, composition).

■ Focus RM efforts on growing rather than maintaining relationships, because "relationship maintenance" often leads to decline and represents a poorly performing relationship state. If unable to grow the relationship, shifting to an efficient transactional format may generate the highest returns (i.e., avoids too much RM, which leads to unwanted customer costs and relational debts).

strong customer relationships. Typically, interpersonal relationships between customers and boundary spanners affect customer behaviors more than do the customers' relationship with the selling firm. To take advantage of the strong effect of interpersonal relationships, *sellers should assign a dedicated contact person to customers,* even if the customers often deal with other boundary spanners or multiple channels. For example, if a customer calls and the dedicated contact person is not available, the nonassigned call-center employees first should acknowledge they are filling in and give customers the option of holding until their dedicated person is available or of leaving a message. (For example, although inbound calls rarely go to the specific rep, the Vanguard mutual fund company assigns all "flagship" customers a dedicated representative and phone number.) Outgoing calls, direct mail, and up- or cross-selling efforts also should be from the assigned contact person. Even web-based interfaces can reference the dedicated call person (e.g., with a picture) or give an option for e-mailing the dedicated contact person. For example, Alaskan Airlines has added a new online assistant, with a picture, name, and female voice, to web pages so customers can ask open-ended questions.

Many key drivers of customer relationships (e.g., expertise, communication, similarity) revolve around boundary spanners; thus, *sellers should focus the largest portion of RM investments on selecting, training, and motivating boundary-spanning employees.* Firms selling luxury, technical, or complex products and most services should recognize that expensive advertising, loyalty points, and rebate programs designed to build customer relationships may be wasteful, from a relationship viewpoint, if they offer poor interactions with contact employees. Firms like Nordstrom, Vanguard, and Starbucks all recognize this point and expend significant efforts to ensure their boundary-spanning personal are effective.

Relationship marketing investments dedicated to specific programs should be allocated primarily to social and structural programs rather than financial programs. Social programs appear to generate the highest returns, even though the boundary spanner often owns the resulting relationship; structural programs also pay off and enhance relationships between the customer and the selling firm. Structural RM programs should target high-volume, existing, or growing customers, because a larger sales volume supports implementation costs and often provides more value to customers with high-frequency interaction. In contrast, firms should minimize their proactive use of financial RM programs (e.g., price reductions, rebates) and instead consider these programs only as price/volume discounts or competitive responses. Most financial programs simply cannot generate positive short-term returns or build long-term relational loyalty. This point clearly is recognized by many firms that are scaling back their many financially based RM programs (e.g., Borders, most airline and credit card companies).

Boundary spanners should have allocation control over most social programs but not over structural and financial programs. Too much allocation control for boundary spanners can create a misallocation among customers and prevent the firm from managing perceptions of responsibility for relationship benefits. In some cases, boundary spanners might undermine the effectiveness of RM programs or steer relationship benefits toward themselves, at the expense of the selling firm. If boundary spanners turn over frequently, sellers should increase consistency, reallocate spending from social to structural programs, and reduce boundary spanners' discretionary control over RM programs.

Those RM programs focused on increasing the amount, frequency, and quality of communication with customers are especially effective and should be initiated early in the relationship lifecycle because communication drives relationship quality and future relationship growth (relational velocity). Developing early communication processes pays multiple dividends. Not only does communication increase relationship quality immediately and over time, but effective communication also helps resolve or prevent corrosive conflict and uncover potential value-creating opportunities. Developing parallel communication channels with varying levels of "touch" and the ability to deal with complex issues may be valuable, but customers typically want responses through the same channel they use to generate their inquiry. For example, RM investments that help customers learn how to use different communication channels (e.g., web- or phone-based information sources), without forcing them into that channel, enable customers to choose the channel that best matches their needs, which improves communication and potentially saves costs.

To understand the effectiveness of RM efforts, *firms should measure their relational assets on an ongoing basis.* Such measures should recognize the multidimensional aspects of customer relationships (e.g., quality, breadth, composition, growth/velocity), and metrics can provide feedback to individual boundary spanners or teams (e.g., input to compensation and bonuses). For interfirm relationships, sellers should capture both the breadth (number of contacts) and composition (authority and diversity) of their customer contact portfolio and focus their efforts on any identified weaknesses. For example, as occurs in many customer satisfaction surveys, if the measure of relationship quality asks an informant to complete a survey, the results may be misleading, especially because the measure provides little insight into how many different relational ties bind the two firms or whether the existing contacts can influence key decisions at the customer firm. In many cases, relational velocity and lifecycle stage measures provide a leading indicator of the future state of the relationship because customers in stagnant or mature relationships may require new RM tactics. If the customer no longer requires a relationship, the seller should either move that customer to a more transactional, low-cost interface or reinvigorate the exchange with new offerings, new personnel, or other changes. Continuing to invest RM efforts in customers that no longer value the relationship is inefficient and may even be detrimental to the exchange.

In addition to monitoring external customer relationships, *sellers should conduct internally focused RM audits to verify that their organizational elements*

*Relationship velocity and lifecycle stage are leading
indicators of the future state of the exchange.*

(firm strategy, leadership, culture, structures, and control) and business processes align with their RM objectives. Expending resources to build and maintain
customer relationships will be ineffective if other aspects of the firm's business
undermine those very efforts. Organizational elements that hinder boundary spanners' motivation and capability to build trust with customers are probably the most
detrimental. A seller's hiring, compensation, training, and support systems are
especially critical, and its culture has a pervasive influence on many aspects of its
interaction with customers. Sellers should take special care to ensure that internal
RM policies and programs are flexible enough to allow boundary spanners to
adapt RM activities to their customers' relationship orientations.

How to Adapt and Target Relationship Marketing

*To enhance the effectiveness of RM, sellers should actively target investments
toward customers with a high relationship orientation (need and desire for a relationship).* Not all customers desire strong relationships; in some cases, they perceive RM activities as a waste of time, unwanted hassle, or extra cost. These customers often shift to transactionally oriented sellers to avoid relational involvement. In one B2B study, customers with a low relationship orientation stated
they would shift 21% of their business to another supplier with similar products if the transactions were completely automated and the salespeople were no
longer involved. Many firms allocate their RM resources to their biggest customers or those with the most potential, which seems to make sense but also
ignores the customer's perspective. Understanding whether the customer needs
or wants a relationship with the seller or boundary spanner is critical. In some
cases, a customer may be receptive regardless of the situation, but typically customers tend to be more relationally oriented and open to relationship building
when they face some risk, uncertainty, or dependence in the exchange process
or are very involved with or motivated about the product or service category. In
these situations, customers find the expertise, added flexibility, and risk-reduc-
tion benefits of a relationship valuable and likely welcome the seller's relational efforts.

*Sellers should leverage RM investments by designing programs that increase
customers' perceptions of the seller's free will, benevolence, risk, and cost in provid-*

ing the RM benefit. A customer's gratitude toward the seller in response to receiving some RM benefit depends on the perception of the deposition of that benefit. Those RM benefits that everyone receives, that are in response to a customer's request, that are given to match a competitor's offer, or that are built into the overall product or service offering generate little gratitude or need to reciprocate. Ideally, all programs should retain some random or discretionary elements because very structured quid pro quo programs tend to be integrated into the overall value proposition and therefore lose their ability to promote relationships (e.g., most airline loyalty points programs), just as salesperson motivation from a sales incentive drops once that salesperson comes to expect the incentive as part of his or her compensation package. Thus, sellers can generate higher returns from a given program by carefully structuring and designing the delivery of the program.

Relationship marketing programs should include some discretionary or random element; otherwise benefits may be integrated into the overall value proposition and no longer promote relationships.

In addition to exploiting the impact of delivery, *a seller can leverage RM investments by providing a benefit when the customer's need is the highest and the benefit provides the most value.* Although the cost of the program to the seller increases customer gratitude, so does the value provided by the benefit; thus boundary spanners should receive some discretion and guidelines regarding when they may immediately solve a customer's problem or provide some RM benefit. The previous two practices can be integrated in an example: consider the level of gratitude and likelihood of future reciprocation felt by a business traveler who has accumulated miles by following the program rules and therefore can upgrade the entire family to first class on an international flight. Compare those levels to a family who receives a spontaneous upgrade on the same flight in appreciation for their patronage in the past. The airline could target this latter program toward high-volume customers who often pay full-fare business rates or fly highly competitive routes, which increases the likelihood that the customer has opportunities to reciprocate.

Designing programs to generate high levels of gratitude is important, but returns appear only if customers act on these feelings. Thus, *sellers should give customers opportunities to reciprocate soon after providing them with an RM benefit (not quid pro quo), which takes advantage of high levels of gratitude, prevents guilt rationalization, and leads to reciprocity norms.* A customer's feeling of gratefulness toward a seller ultimately will decay and, in the worst case scenario, generate feelings of guilt, which customers try to relieve by rationalizing why they did not reciprocate (e.g., assigning a negative motive to the seller). In the airline example discussed above, the airline could contact the frequent flier with an offer promising that if he or she books multiple flights over the next six months, the airline will provide a token discount for upgrades. This offer would provide the flier an opportunity to act on any feelings of gratitude and lead to reciprocity norms between the seller and customer. However, the airline absolutely cannot refer to the previous RM benefit or structure the request as a means for the customer to pay for benefits received. Research shows that people often reciprocate far in excess of the value received and continue to feel grateful.

Sellers should focus RM efforts on growing rather than maintaining relationships, because relationship maintenance often leads to decline and reflects a poorly performing relationship. If unable to grow a relationship, shifting to an efficient, transactional format may generate the highest returns for a seller. Therefore, RM investments should be targeted and adapted according to the relationship stage, such that investments are concentrated in the early growth stages when customers are more receptive to relationship building and competitive rivalry may be lower. Later in the relationship lifecycle, as the relationship matures, existing structural linkages and communication processes provide the seller with a competitive barrier. During the maintenance stage, RM investments should be cut back to match the customers' needs, and sellers should explore opportunities to launch new products or services or expand the exchange to new contacts to shift the customer back into a growth trajectory. This guidance parallels Blattberg and Deighton's (1996, p. 144) recommendation to develop "different marketing plans—or even build two different marketing organizations—for acquisition and retention efforts," a suggestion that recognizes that fundamentally different relationship marketing strategies are needed across the various lifecycle stages.

8
Future Research Directions and Topics

In the past two decades, the significant research efforts dedicated to relationship marketing have illuminated and clarified various issues in RM theory and practice. But those efforts also reveal the incredibly complex and contingent ways in which relationships affect behavior and performance. Therefore, whereas the preceding chapters paint a picture of what research has revealed about relationship marketing, this chapter summarizes and outlines potential future research directions and topics.

Measuring Relational Assets

To provide a more complete view of relationships and their meaning, further research must expand the constructs used to measure a firm's relational assets. Commitment and trust continue to play critical roles, but the scope of investigations also should expand to capture other performance-relevant relationship features, including gratitude, exchange efficiency, equity, relational norms, relational velocity, lifecycle stage, or reciprocity. In interfirm relationships, potential factors also include breadth, composition, strength, and efficacy. In particular, current research lacks a good measure of reciprocity between exchange partners, even though this element may represent "the core of marketing relationships" (Bagozzi 1995, p. 275). As the span and reach of relational constructs expand, so should the scope of research enabling marketers to investigate potential interactions among relational constructs and identify relational synergies.

Relationship Antecedents

Existing research supports the influence of a relatively small set of antecedents (i.e., relationship marketing activities) on the formation of relational assets. Additional research should expand this set. For example, what relative importance does a selling firm's organizational design (e.g., leadership, strategy, culture, control, and structure) have on its ability to execute RM effectively? Because conflict harms relational assets, more effort also should go into understanding how firms can remedy conflict-laden relationships, especially as they pertain to service or relationship recovery strategies. Even communication, which affects both the level and growth (relational velocity) of relational assets, requires more investigation to gain a full understanding of its role in RM.

In response to recent findings that expand the number of relational attributes (e.g., breadth, depth, reciprocity, efficacy, gratitude) that represent a firm's relational assets, further research should isolate the relative efficacy of antecedents across different relational constructs. For example, which RM programs tend to result in exchange inefficiencies? Recall that customers with a low RO likely consider interpersonal RM inefficient because it creates a reciprocity-based obligation to respond, and they prefer electronic or more impersonal RM. Extant research focuses mostly on the seller's RM benefits and costs; more research effort instead should investigate the *customer's* benefits and costs because understanding how these features vary across relational interfaces would clarify the tradeoffs associated with relational versus transactional selling approaches. Interfirm researchers also should identify effective RM strategies that work across relational drivers. For example, group social events, training seminars, and telemarketing or direct-mail campaigns might expand the breadth or density of relational contacts by generating new prospects, whereas one-on-one social programs and similarity between boundary spanners could help build relationship quality; using senior executives or experts may work best to improve relationship composition and penetrate new areas within customer firms.

Extant research focuses mostly on the seller's RM benefits and costs; more research should instead investigate the customer's benefits and costs.

Relationship Outcomes

If research does not expand the range of performance outcomes it studies to identify RM's overall impact, it runs the risk of systematically underestimating the true effects. Sales growth, diversity, volatility, share of wallet, retention, upselling, and cross-buying all might provide more complete pictures of sales-based RM outcomes. But research also should move beyond sales-based outcomes to consider profitability measures such as price premiums, selling and acquisition costs, lifetime value, and ROI. Finally, in the field of innovation research, existing models should integrate relational constructs to gain insight into the potentially beneficial effects of RM on knowledge acquisition and new product development and launch. Specifically, knowledge-based measures—such as patents, time-to-market, and new product success—could help identify the mechanisms through which relationships and RM help firms innovate.

Outcomes also feature a temporal element, but few studies sufficiently isolate the payoff cycle and longevity of RM programs; instead, they rely on cross-sectional data or simply measure RM effects a year later. Yet strong interpersonal relationships and structural RM programs could extend for many years, whereas loyalty points or similar programs likely have only short-term effects.

The true impact of RM on knowledge acquisition and innovation is not understood.

Multilevel and Intergroup Relationships

When RM studies pertain to groups of decision makers (e.g., buying centers, households), they must consider both the multilevel nature of the relational ties and the effects of group decision processes. Differential judgment processes operate for interpersonal relationships (i.e., an online model) compared with person-to-firm relationships (i.e., a recall model) and can alter how firms simultaneously build and maintain multilevel relationships. For example, a customer–salesperson relationship may be able to withstand a service failure when the customer–selling firm relationship might not. In addition, when selling firms embrace well-defined corporate cultures, integrated selling teams, and frequently rotated, tightly scripted, closely regimented salesforces their relationships with customers may be more significant than the relationships between customers and salespeople. In all cases, greater understanding of the differences between individual and group decision making would result from additional studies in other cultures and marketing contexts (e.g., services, retail, online). Social psychology literature pertaining to group decision making could offer extensive information about how marketing decisions are made. For example, it offers norm persistence as a means to understand how the newest employee of the customer firm assumes an ongoing relationship with a supplier.

Negative Effects of Relationship Marketing

By focusing perhaps too narrowly on the beneficial effects of RM, previous studies may have missed some negative effects, such as cognitive inertia, routine rigidity, or reduced environmental screening—which limit the level of flexibility and creativity among exchange partners—that result from strong relational ties. By focusing too much on how relationships help sellers, research fails to consider how these same relational effects might negatively influence a salesperson, for example, to offer a price below established pricing levels to a customer with which they have a strong relationship. From a customer perspective, the implication that some try to avoid interpersonal relationships suggests that norms of reciprocity result in high-maintenance interactions. Even if that customer, out of courtesy or reciprocity, permits the salesperson to visit, deliver unwanted RM benefits, or perform insignificant services, the unnecessary costs and lack of relational benefit these efforts imply may prompt the customer to seek a less demanding interaction with a competitor. This dark side of strong interpersonal relationships interactions demands much more investigation.

More effort is needed to understand how RM can negatively affect performance through inefficiencies, cognitive rigidity, and seller-side relationship effects (price erosion).

Relationship Dynamics

Understanding the dynamic nature of relationships provides an important topic for further research. Relational velocity appears to predict performance better than measures of the level of relational constructs, which suggests that marketers must have a better understanding of performance differences among relationship lifecycle stages, as well as the appropriate RM strategies to use in each of those stages. Existing research considers, of course, trust and commitment, but other interorganizational constructs may reveal unique natural responses or developmental cycles. For example, gratitude probably has a relatively short lifecycle, which implies sellers can collect on feelings of gratitude during only a short window of opportunity after an RM investment. Once this window closes, the performance-enhancing benefits of gratitude likely dissolve, unless the seller has initiated a cycle of reciprocation that strengthens long-term reciprocity norms.

Evaluating the impact of interfirm relational drivers on exchange outcomes across the relationship lifecycle also could provide a fruitful line of inquiry. In early stages, bond quality may be most critical, because initial bonds plant the seeds for interfirm norms. Yet during the growth stage, sellers want to enhance sales penetration, which requires action by diverse decision makers; therefore relationship composition may be the most critical component.

Finally, as relationships mature and sellers shift from a focus on share expansion to share protection, relationship breadth could create a web of ties that bar customer switching and competitive pressures. According to network research, "densely tied networks produce strong constraints," which supports the premise that relationship breadth may constrain customer actions (Rowley 1997, p. 897). Therefore, additional research should consider how suppliers might supplement their known weaknesses in relationship breadth or composition by leveraging channel members' contact portfolios. It also might investigate the underlying or mediating mechanisms that clarify how relationship breadth and composition influence performance.

Relationship Marketing Boundary Conditions and Context Effects

Most RM research employs a main effects model, but most effects in that model depend on exchange-specific conditions, which means significant, unexplained heterogeneity across the main effects (Palmatier et al. 2006). Several moderating variables, including customer, seller, and environmental variables that might either undermine or leverage RM investments, probably operate in accordance with the specific linkage or relational driver being investigated. For example, the seller's brand strength, environmental uncertainty, and customer dependence likely affect the influence of relationship quality on performance, whereas the customer decision-making processes, team selling, and industry maturity may moderate the effects of relationship breadth. Further research should determine when RM is most effective and the best ways to adapt RM strategies; such information, in combination with the extensive data available from CRM systems, could enhance one-to-one, customized relationship marketing. In turn, this enhancement could help ensure that CRM technology investments actually pay off.

In particular, two global trends are altering the conditions for RM. First, populations everywhere, but especially in developed countries, are aging, which means companies need to adjust their RM strategies to appeal to older consumers. Most older people care more about relationship ties, employ simplified decision heuristics, avoid complexity, and gain more pleasure from interpersonal relationships, so marketers may want to increase their RM investments in this age group, assuming further research supports this proposition. Second, the ever increasing frequency with which customers employ multiple channels (Web, phone, retail, salesperson) to interact with sellers means that marketers require greater insight into how to build effective relationships in this context and which methods they might use to transfer relational assets across interfaces and channels.

Relationship Marketing Theory

Various theoretical perspectives help inform RM; additional research should acknowledge these insights, investigate how well each theory predicts outcomes, and integrate the alternative perspectives into a holistic RM model. This last effort will prove particularly difficult because it must confront the bias against conceptual models based on multiple theoretical perspectives. But some of the most promising theoretical frameworks may feature the resource-based view, the knowledge-based view, and social network theory; integrating other network variables into interorganizational research could be even more beneficial. For example, to capture which characteristics of interfirm exchanges really improve performance, researchers could address network centrality, network timing, network multiplicity, and network resources.

At the same time, RM research cannot dismiss the significance of key theories and findings in social psychology, sociology, anthropology, and evolutionary psychology, disciplines that investigate the role and impact of individual and group interactions and that therefore can provide great insight into marketing phenomena. Social psychology already shows that guilt drives behavior; relationship marketing should use this insight to determine its impact in a marketing setting. A sense of guilt as a result of an unreciprocated relationship benefit could enhance performance in the short run, as the customer attempts to relieve that guilt, but it also could have an ultimately negative effect if the customer eventually must rationalize their failure to reciprocate. On the flip side of this coin, what happens when customers perceive that sellers have violated reciprocity norms? Do they seek to punish the seller/violator? Applying thin-slice judgments (conditions of little information and time) to relationship building could clarify how customers form judgments about relationship partners and inform the first-impressions phenomenon.

Alternative Research Methods

These recommended research directions often require alternative methods. Cross-sectional data, collected from surveys in business markets, will continue to be important because they support large-scale, holistic models based on latent constructs. But for integrating new constructs from other disciplines (e.g., gratitude, guilt), experimental approaches and mixed methods may be more helpful. Furthermore, more and more RM programs appear in consumer markets, but most research continues to take place primarily in B2B contexts. Investigating relationship dynamics means collecting multiple periods of longitudinal data and using latent growth models or other longitudinal analysis techniques. Finally, extant research contains a wealth of samples from Western cultures but few multicultural studies. Therefore, increased efforts to replicate and compare RM conceptual models across divergent societies could identify appropriate ways to adapt RM strategies according to specific cultural attributes.

Glossary

Commitment	An enduring desire to maintain a valued relationship
Communication	Amount, frequency, and quality of information shared between exchange partners
Conflict	Overall level of disagreement between exchange partners
Contingency theory	Theory arguing that the effectiveness of a firm's actions depends on its fit with structural and contextual factors
Cooperative behaviors	Coordinated, complementary actions between partners to achieve a mutual goal
Customer relationship management	Managerially relevant application of relationship marketing across an organization focused on customers, which leverages information technology to achieve performance objectives
Customer relationship orientation	Desire to engage in a strong relationship with a current or potential partner
Dependence on seller	Customer's evaluation of the value of seller-provided resources for which few alternatives are available from other sellers
Entitativity	Degree to which a party exhibits coherence, unity, or consistency
Financial RM programs	Programs that are built by providing economic benefits in exchange for past or future customer loyalty, examples of which include special discounts, free

products to generate incremental sales, or other incentives easily converted to financial savings such as free shipping or extended payment terms

Gratitude

Feelings of gratefulness, thankfulness, or appreciation toward an exchange partner for benefits received

Industry relational norms

Norms reflecting the value placed on customer–supplier relationships within the industry

Interaction frequency

Number of interactions or number of interactions per unit of time between exchange partners

Knowledge-based outcome measures

Measures that may represent an important outcome of strong customer–seller relationships that is not captured in the pure financial measures, because customer relational behaviors may provide sellers with insight into new markets, help them uncover new product opportunities, enable them to beta test and refine new product concepts, and accelerate adoption of new product launches; strong relationships also may influence sellers' financial performance in ways that typical financial metrics cannot isolate (e.g., number of patents, number of new products)

Latent growth curve modeling

Mathematical modeling that studies the time-varying trajectories of constructs (variables)

Latent growth parameters

Level, velocity, and acceleration factors that explain observed growth trajectories

Lifecycle stage

Qualitative path-dependent phases through which a relationship transitions. Relationships typically expand during the exploration and buildup stages, peak, remain relatively flat during the maturity stage, and weaken during the decline stage.

Marketing

Organizational function and a set of processes for creating, communicating, and delivering value to customers and for managing customer relationships in ways that benefit the organization and its stake-holders

Product category involvement	The importance of a product category to the customer, which may stem from personal-, firm-, or role-related needs, values, and interests
Product dependence	Customer's need to maintain a relationship with a selling firm to acquire a specific product with the greatest efficiency
Reciprocity norms	Internalized patterns of behaviors and feelings that regulate the balance of obligations between two exchange partners
Relational control element	The system in place to monitor, incentivize, or punish employees as a result of their customer interface activities
Relational loyalty	The likelihood that the customer provides the seller with an advantage or benefits in the exchange process because of their relational ties
Relational velocity	Magnitude and direction of the rate of change in the quality of a relationship
Relational-centric systems	Degree to which a firm's evaluation systems, compensation reward programs, and policies promote strong customer–supplier relationships
Relationship benefits	Benefits received, including time saving, convenience, companionship, and improved decision making from a customer–seller relationship
Relationship breadth	Number of relational ties with an exchange partner
Relationship composition	Decision-making capability of the relational contacts at an exchange partner
Relationship duration	Length of time that the relationship between the exchange partners has existed

Relationship efficacy	Ability of a relationship to achieve desired objectives
Relationship investments	Seller's investment of time, effort, spending, and resources focused on building a stronger relationship
Relationship marketing	The process of identifying, developing, maintaining, and terminating relational exchanges with the purpose of enhancing performance
Relationship proneness	A person's basic tendency to engage in relationships
Relationship satisfaction	Customer's affective state toward a relationship
Relationship strength	Ability of a relationship to withstand stress and/or conflict
Resource dependence theory	Theory suggesting that a party can manage its dependence on its exchange partners by building relationships with those partners
Sales-based outcome measures	The most common financial performance metrics, which recognize that relational behaviors (e.g., reciprocation, reduced search, last look) can increase or minimize drops in sales revenue; they may take many forms, including annual sales growth, sales diversity (number of different products and services sold to a customer), sales volatility (variability in sales over time), and share of wallet (sales penetration for a specific customer).
Salesperson competence	Salesperson's capabilities or expertise across a range of relevant tasks
Salesperson-owned loyalty	Customer's intention to perform behaviors that signal motivation to maintain a relationship specifically with the focal salesperson
Seller expertise	Knowledge, experience, and overall competency of seller
Seller-owned loyalty	Loyalty to the seller specifically, independent of the salesperson, that is based in elements that the seller as an organization controls or in other employees of the seller with whom the customer interacts

Similarity	Commonality in appearance, lifestyle, and status between individual boundary spanners, or similar cultures, values, and goals between buying and selling organizations
Social RM programs	Programs that focus on personalizing the customer relationship, conveying special status to the buyer through social engagements such as meals and sporting events, and the provision of frequent, customized, or personalized communication
Structural RM programs	Programs that increase productivity and/or efficiency for customers through investments that customers likely would not make themselves, examples of which include electronic order-processing interface, customized packaging, and other policy or procedural changes
Synergistic loyalty	Loyalty engendered neither by the seller apart from the salesperson nor by the salesperson individually, but by the benefits to the customer that the seller–salesperson association generates together
Trust	Confidence in an exchange partner's reliability and integrity
Word-of-mouth (WOM)	The likelihood that a customer comments positively about a seller to another potential customer (whether inside or outside the firm). Because WOM behaviors are not masked by high switching costs and lack of time or motivation, they sometimes appear as indicators of customer loyalty.

Appendix

Table A1
Summary of Illustrative Research on Relationship Dynamics and

Reference	Lifecycle Stages
Dwyer, Schurr, and Oh (1987)	Awareness, exploration, expansion, commitment, dissolution
Heide (1994)	Initiation, maintenance, termination
Wilson (1995)	Partner selection, defining purpose, setting relationship boundaries, creating relationship value, relationship maintenance
Lewicki and Bunker (1996)	Stage 1 (calculus- and deterrence-based trust), stage 2 (knowledge-based trust), stage 3 (identification-based trust)
Rosseau et al. (1998)	Early (dominated by calculative and institutional trust), middle, later (dominated by relational trust)
Jap and Ganesan (2000)	Exploration, buildup, maturity, decline
Hibbard et al. (2001)	Quartile 1 (age = 1–96 months), quartile 2 (age = 97–160 months), quartile 3 (age = 161–236 months), quartile 4 (age = 237+ months)
Jap and Anderson (2007)	Compared Dwyer, Schurr, and Oh (1987) to Ring and Van de Ven (1994)

Lifecycle Effects

Empirical Approach	Expectations/Findings Regarding Relational Variables
Conceptual	Bilateral communication, goal congruence, trust, and joint satisfaction move in concert
Full framework not tested	Mutual dependence leads to bilateral (relational) governance
Ethnographic	Social bonds, mutual goals, satisfaction, trust, and cooperation move in concert
Conceptual	Experience with partner causes the basis of trust to evolve from calculative to knowledge to identification
Conceptual	Calculative trust is replaced over time by relational trust
Cross-sectional, age cohorts	Reciprocity, bilateral investments, relational norms, and commitment move in concert
Cross-sectional, age as a covariate	Trust, commitment, communication, shared values, and mutual dependence move in concert; relationship between variables and outcomes generally diminish over time
Cross-sectional, age cohorts	Most relationships follow Dwyer, Schurr, and Oh's (1987) predictions; those that cycle have worse performance. Goal congruence, information exchange, harmony, and trust move in concert

Table A2
Constructs, Definitions, and Example Items for Measuring Relational

Constructs	Definitions
Relationship quality	Caliber of relational bonds with an exchange partner
Commitment	An enduring desire to maintain a valued relationship
Trust	Confidence in an exchange partner's reliability and integrity
Relationship satisfaction	Customer's affective state toward a relationship
Gratitude	Feelings of gratefulness, thankfulness, or appreciation toward an exchange partner for benefits received
Reciprocity norms	Internalized patterns of behaviors and feelings that regulate the balance of obligations between two exchange partners

Relationship Dynamics

Relational velocity	Magnitude and direction of the rate of change in the relational quality of a relationship

Assets

Representative Measurement Items

Composite of measures of component constructs

I am [My firm is] willing "to go the extra mile" to work with this salesperson [selling firm]. I feel [My firm feels] committed to the relationship with this salesperson [selling firm]. I [My firm] would work hard to maintain my [our] relationship with this salesperson [selling firm].

This salesperson [selling firm] gives me a feeling [us feelings] of trust. This salesperson [selling firm] is always honest. This salesperson [selling firm] is trustworthy.

I am [My firm is] pleased with the relationship with this salesperson [selling firm]. I am [My firm is] happy with the relationship with this salesperson [selling firm]. I am [My firm is] satisfied with the relationship I [we] have with this salesperson [selling firm].

I feel [My firm feels] grateful to this salesperson [selling firm]. I feel [My firm feels] thankful to this salesperson [selling firm]. I feel [My firm feels] obligated to this salesperson [selling firm].

I [My firm] would help this salesperson [selling firm] if there was a need or problem in the future. In the long term the benefits this salesperson [selling firm] and I [my firm] receive from each other will balance out. Buying from this salesperson makes [selling firm makes] me [us] feel good. I [My firm] would expect this salesperson [selling firm] to help me [us] in the future.

My firm's relationship with this salesperson [selling firm] is strengthening.

I think the quality of my [firm's] relationship with this salesperson [firm] will continue to improve in the future.

My [firm's] relationship with this salesperson [selling firm] is growing over time.

A2 Constructs, Definitions, and Example Items for Measuring Relational Assets
continued from page 109

Lifecycle stage	Qualitative path-dependent phases through which a relationship transitions. Relationships typically expand during the exploration and buildup stages, peak and remain relatively flat during the maturity stage, and weaken during the decline stage.

Interfirm Relationships

Relationship breadth	Number of relational ties with an exchange partner
Relationship composition	Decision-making capability of the relational contacts at an exchange partner
Relationship strength	Ability of a relationship to withstand stress and/or conflict (relational quality x relational breadth)
Relationship efficacy	Ability of a relationship to achieve desired objectives (relational quality x relational composition)

Notes: All items are seven-point scales with "strongly disagree" and "strongly agree" as anchors, unless otherwise noted.

Exploration: You both are in the very early stage of discovering and evaluating compatibility, integrity, and performance of the other party.

Buildup: You both are receiving increasing benefits from the relationship, and the level of trust and satisfaction is growing in such a way that you are increasingly willing to commit to a long-term relationship.

Maturity: You both have an ongoing, long-term relationship in which both parties receive acceptable levels of satisfaction and benefits from the relationship.

Decline: One or both of you have begun to experience dissatisfaction and are evaluating alternatives, contemplating relationship termination, or beginning to end the relationship.

How many different relationship ties are there among employees at [selling firm] and your firm? (number)

[Selling firm] knows the key decision makers at our firm. [Selling firm] has relationships with the important gatekeepers at our firm. [Selling firm] deals with the important decision makers in our company. [Selling firm] has contacts with what percent of the key decision makers at your firm? (percentage) [Selling firm] has contacts in how many different functional departments in your firm? (number)

Our relationship with [selling firm] allows us to easily adapt to change. In total, I think my firm's relationship with [selling firm] is very strong. A single conflict or disagreement would have little effect on our overall relationship with [selling firm].

[Selling firm] does a good job working with people at our firm to reach its goals. [Selling firm] is very effective at selling to our firm. Our relationship with [selling firm] allows them to be very effective at working with our firm.

Brackets "[ ]" represent required substitutions to make the measurement items correspond to the target of the customer's relationship (e.g., salesperson versus [selling firm] and whether the customer is acting as a respondent or an [informant]).

Table A3
Relationship Marketing Typologies

Proposed Typology	Criteria for Typology
Financial, social, and structural bonds	Relationship marketing can be distinguished on the basis of the type of customer–seller bond or linkage. Proposes that each level or type of bond leads to differences in seller's sustainable competitive advantage and financial performance.
Special treatment (economic and customization), social, and confidence (psychological) benefits	Customers receive three different types of benefits from seller relationship marketing efforts. Sellers may be able to differentiate by focusing relationship marketing efforts toward specific types of programs.
Economic, social, and technical content	Relationships solve problems and/or have functions across three different dimensions or content areas for exchanges between buyers and sellers.
Economic, social, and resource content	Suggests the antecedents to trust and commitment (i.e., relationships) can be captured by three content areas, where cooperation and positive outcomes depend on these categories in a progression from economic to resource and finally social.

Differences among Categories	References
Financial bonds generate least competitive advantage and lowest financial return. Social bonds generate higher returns, and structural bonds with customers lead to the highest financial returns.	Berry 1995; Berry and Parasuraman 1991
Special treatment benefits (economic and customization) are the least important benefit. Social benefits are the next most important, and confidence benefits (i.e., reduced anxiety and higher levels of trustworthiness) are the most important to consumers.	Gwinner, Gremler, and Bitner 1998
Each of these three content areas can lead to unique economic and competitive advantages.	Håkansson and Snehota 2000
Content areas differentially influence various aspects of a relationship, and higher content levels are conditional on lower levels: economic → resource → social	Morgan 2000

Table A4
Illustrative Research Summarizing the Drivers to Customer

Illustrative Research	Theoretical Basis
Anderson and Narus (1991)	Qualitative case-based research
Cannon and Perreault (1999)	Resource dependence theory (Pfeffer and Salancik 1978) and transaction cost economics (Williamson 1985)
De Wulf, Odekerken-Schröder, and Iacobucci (2001)	Based on research suggesting more involved customers have a tendency to be more loyal and that some customers are "psychologically predisposed" to relationships (Christy, Oliver, and Penn 1996)
Dwyer, Schurr, and Oh (1987)	Transaction cost economics (Williamson 1985) and contracting theory (Macneil 1980)
Johnson (1999)	Resource-based view (Barney 1991)
Johnson and Sohi (2001)	Political economies framework (Stern and Reve 1980)
Heide and John (1992)	Transaction cost economics (Williamson 1985), contracting theory, and relational norms (Macaulay 1963; Macneil 1980)
Noordewier, John, and Nevin (1990)	Transaction cost economics (Williamson 1985)

1. This table is based on Palmatier et al. 2008.

Relationship Orientation[1]

Drivers to Relational Orientation	Context
Value to customer, relative dependence, industry norms, and customer's philosophy of doing business	Business-to-business interactions
Dependence, dynamism, complexity of purchase, and importance of product	Business-to-business interactions
Product category involvement and relational proneness	Interactions between food and apparel retailers and consumers
Dependence, uncertainty, exchange efficiency, and social satisfaction	Business-to-business interactions
Dependence, age, flexibility, continuity expectations, and relationship quality	Business-to-business interactions
Relational proclivity	Business-to-business interactions
Transaction-specific investments and dependence	Component suppliers and OEM manufacturers
Uncertainty	Supplier of ball bearings to industrial customers

Table A5
Summary of Measures for Customer Relationship Orientation

Measurement Items

This business transaction requires a close relationship between me and [selling firm] to ensure its success.

A close relationship with [selling firm] is important to my success.

A strong relationship with [selling firm] would be very helpful in buying this product.

I don't need a close relationship with [selling firm] to successfully buy this product. (Reverse)

I believe that a strong relationship with [selling firm] is needed to successfully buy this product.

Notes: All items are seven-point scales with "strongly disagree" and "strongly agree" as anchors, unless otherwise noted. Brackets "[ ]" represent required substitutions to make the measurement items correspond to the target of the customer's relationship (e.g., salesperson versus [selling firm]).

Notes

1. This section of the monograph is based on Palmatier (2007, 2008).

2. Interested readers can refer to Van den Bulte and Wuyts (2007) for additional information on social network theory.

3. The term *customer* is used generically to represent the customer side of the exchange dyad, which could be an individual decision maker (buyer) or customer firm (buying center), whereas *consumer* is used to specifically represent the case of an individual decision maker (not a firm), as in a B2C context.

4. This section of the monograph is based on Palmatier et al. (2006).

5. This section of the monograph is based on Palmatier, Gopalakrishna, and Houston (2006).

6. This section of the monograph is based on Palmatier et al. (2008).

References

Adler, Mitchel G., and N. S. Fagley (2005), "Appreciation: Individual Differences in Finding Value and Meaning as a Unique Predictor of Subjective Well-Being." *Journal of Personality* 73 (February), 79-114.

Alderson, Wroe (1958), "The Analytical Framework for Marketing." In *Proceedings: Conference of Marketing Teachers from Far Western States*, ed. Delbert Duncan, 15-28. Berkeley, Calif.: University of California, Berkeley.

Alderson, Wroe (1965), *Dynamic Marketing Behavior: A Functionalist Theory of Marketing*. Homewood, Ill.: Richard D. Irwin, Inc.

Ambler, Tim, Chris Styles, and Wang Xiucum (1999), "The Effect of Channel Relationships and Guanxi on the Performance of Inter-Province Export Ventures in the People's Republic of China." *International Journal of Research in Marketing* 16 (February), 75–87.

Anderson, Erin, and Barton A. Weitz (1989), "Determinants of Continuity in Conventional Industrial Channel Dyads." *Marketing Science* 8 (Fall), 310–23.

Anderson, Erin, and Barton A. Weitz (1992), "The Use of Pledges to Build and Sustain Commitment in Distribution Channels." *Journal of Marketing Research* 29 (February), 18–34.

Anderson, James C., Håkan Håkansson, and Jan Johanson (1994), "Dyadic Business Relationships Within a Business Network Context." *Journal of Marketing* 58 (October), 1–15.

Anderson, James C., and James A. Narus (1990), "A Model of Distributor Firm and Manufacturer Firm Working Partnerships." *Journal of Marketing* 54 (January), 42–58.

Anderson, James C., and James A. Narus (1991), "Partnering as a Focused Market Strategy." *California Management Review* 33 (Spring), 95–113.

Anderson, James C., and James A. Narus (2004), *Business Market Management: Understanding, Creating, and Delivering Value.* Upper Saddle River, N.J.: Prentice Hall.

Arndt, Johan (1979), "Toward a Concept of Domesticated Markets." *Journal of Marketing* 43 (Fall), 69–75.

Arora, Neeraj, and Greg M. Allenby (1999), "Measuring the Influence of

Individual Preference Structures in Group Decision Making." *Journal of Marketing Research* 36 (November), 476–87.

Bagozzi, Richard P. (1975), "Marketing as Exchange." *Journal of Marketing* 39 (October), 32–9.

Bagozzi, Richard P. (1995), "Reflections on Relationship Marketing in Consumer Markets." *Journal of the Academy of Marketing Science* 23 (4), 272–7.

Barksdale, Hiram C., Jr., Julie T. Johnson, and Munshik Suh (1997), "A Relationship Maintenance Model: A Comparison Between Managed Health Care and Traditional Fee-for-Service." *Journal of Business Research* 40 (3), 237–47.

Barney, Jay B. (1991), "Firm Resources and Competitive Advantage." *Journal of Management* 17 (March), 99–120.

Bartels, Robert (1962), *The Development of Marketing Thought.* Homewood, Ill.: Richard D. Irwin.

Bartlett, Monica Y., and David DeSteno (2006), "Gratitude and Prosocial Behavior." *Psychological Science* 17 (April), 319–25.

Baum, Joel A. C., Tony C. Calabrese, and Brian S. Silverman (2000), "Don't Go It Alone: Alliance Network Composition and Startups' Performance in Canadian Biotechnology." *Strategic Management Journal* 21 (March), 267–94.

Becker, Lawrence C. (1986), *Reciprocity.* New York, N.Y.: Routledge & Kegan Paul.

Bejou, David, and Adrian Palmer (1998), "Service Failure and Loyalty: An Exploratory Empirical Study of Airline Customers." *Journal of Services Marketing* 12, 7–22.

Bendapudi, Neeli, and Leonard L. Berry (1997), "Customers' Motivations for Maintaining Relationships with Service Providers." *Journal of Retailing* 73 (1), 15–37.

Bendapudi, Neeli, and Robert P. Leone (2002), "Managing Business-to-Business Customer Relationships Following Key Contact Employee Turnover in a Vendor Firm." *Journal of Marketing* 66 (April), 83–101.

Bergen, Mark, Shantanu Dutta, and Orville C. Walker, Jr. (1992), "Agency Relationships in Marketing: A Review of the Implications and Applications of Agency and Related Theories." *Journal of Marketing* 56 (July), 1–24.

Berger, Paul D., and Nada I. Nasr (1998), "Customer Lifetime Value: Marketing Models and Applications." *Journal of Interactive Marketing* 12 (Winter), 17–30.

Berry, Leonard L. (1983), "Relationship Marketing." In *Emerging Perspectives in Services Marketing,* eds. Leonard L. Berry, G. L. Shostack, and G. D. Upah,

25–8. Chicago, Ill.: American Marketing Association.

Berry, Leonard L. (1995), "Relationship Marketing of Services—Growing Interest, Emerging Perspectives." *Journal of the Academy of Marketing Science* 23 (4), 236–45.

Berry, Leonard L. (1996), "Retailers with a Future." *Marketing Management* 5 (Spring), 39–46.

Berry, Leonard L., and A. Parasuraman (1991), *Marketing Services: Competing Through Quality*. New York, N.Y.: Free Press.

Bettencourt, Lance A. (1997), "Customer Voluntary Performance: Customers as Partners in Service Delivery." *Journal of Retailing* 73 (3), 383–406.

Blattberg, Robert C., and John Deighton (1996), "Manage Marketing by the Customer Equity Test." *Harvard Business Review* 74 (July/August), 136–44.

Blau, Peter (1964), *Exchange and Power in Social Life*. New York, N.Y.: John Wiley & Sons.

Boles, James S., Julie T. Johnson, and Hiram C. Barksdale, Jr. (2000), "How Salespeople Build Quality Relationships: A Replication and Extension." *Journal of Business Research* 48 (1), 75–81.

Bollen, Kenneth A., and Patrick J. Curran (2006), *Latent Curve Models: A Structural Equation Perspective*. Hoboken, N.J.: John Wiley & Sons.

Bolton, Ruth N., P. K. Kannan, and Matthew D. Bramlett (2000), "Implications of Loyalty Programs Membership and Service Experiences for Customer Retention and Value." *Journal of the Academy of Marketing Sciences* 28 (Winter), 95–108.

Bolton, Ruth N., Amy K. Smith, and Janet Wagner (2003), "Striking the Right Balance: Designing Service to Enhance Business-to-Business Relationships." *Journal of Service Research* 5 (May), 271–91.

Bonoma, Thomas V., and Wesley J. Johnston (1978), "The Social Psychology of Industrial Buying and Selling." *Industrial Marketing Management* 7 (August), 213–24.

Borgatti, Stephen P., and Pacey C. Foster (2003), "The Network Paradigm in Organizational Research: A Review and Topology." *Journal of Management* 29 (6), 991–1013.

Boulding, William, Richard Staelin, Michael Ehret, and Wesley J. Johnston (2005), "A Customer Relationship Management Roadmap: What Is Known, Potential Pitfalls, and Where to Go." *Journal of Marketing* 69 (October), 155–66.

Boyle, Richard, and Phillip Bonacich (1970), "The Development of Trust and Mistrust in Mixed-Motive Games." *Sociometry* 33 (June), 123–39.

Brown, Rupert (2000), *Group Processes: Dynamics Within and Between Groups*. Malden, Mass.: Blackwell Publishing Ltd.

Bucklin, Louis P., and Sanjit Sengupta (1993), "Organizing Successful Co-Marketing Alliances." *Journal of Marketing* 57 (April), 32–46.

Burt, Ronald S. (1992), *Structural Holes: The Social Structure of Competition.* Cambridge, Mass.: Harvard University Press.

Campbell, Donald T. (1958), "Common Fate, Similarity, and Other Indices of the Status of Aggregates of Persons as Social Entities." *Behavioral Science* 3 (1), 14–25.

Cannon, Joseph P., Ravi S. Achrol, and Gregory T. Gundlach (2000), "Contracts, Norms, and Plural Form Governance." *Journal of the Academy of Marketing Science* 28 (Spring), 180–94.

Cannon, Joseph P., and William D. Perreault, Jr. (1999), "Buyer-Seller Relationships in Business Markets." *Journal of Marketing Research* 36 (November), 439–60.

Cao, Yong, and Thomas S. Gruca (2005), "Reducing Adverse Selection Through Customer Relationship Management." *Journal of Marketing* 69 (October), 219–29.

Celly, Kirti Sawhney, and Gary L. Frazier (1996), "Outcome-Based and Behavior-Based Coordination Efforts in Channel Relationships." *Journal of Marketing Research* 33 (May), 200–10.

Chase, Richard B., and David A. Tansik (1983), "The Customer Contact Model for Organizational Design." *Management Science* 29 (9), 1037–50.

Chen, Yuxin, and Ganesh Iyer (2002), "Consumer Addressability and Customized Pricing." *Marketing Science* 21 (Spring), 197–208.

Christy, Richard, Gordon Oliver, and Joe Penn (1996), "Relationship Marketing in Consumer Markets." *Journal of Marketing Management* 12 (1–3), 175–87.

Cialdini, Robert B. (2001), *Influence: Science and Practice.* Boston, Mass.: Allyn and Bacon.

Cialdini, Robert B., and Kelton V. L. Rhoads (2001), "Human Behavior and the Marketplace." *Marketing Research* 13 (3), 8–13.

Colgate, Mark R., and Peter J. Danaher (2000), "Implementing a Customer Relationship Strategy: The Asymmetric Impact of Poor Versus Excellent Execution." *Journal of the Academy of Marketing Science* 28 (3), 375–87.

Crosby, Lawrence A., Kenneth R. Evans, and Deborah Cowles (1990), "Relationship Quality in Services Selling: An Interpersonal Influence Perspective." *Journal of Marketing* 54 (July), 68–81.

Crosby, Lawrence A., and Nancy Stephens (1987), "Effects of Relationship Marketing on Satisfaction, Retention, and Prices in the Life Insurance Industry." *Journal of Marketing Research* 24 (November), 404–11.

Dahl, Darren W., Heather Honea, and Rajesh V. Manchanda (2003), "The

Nature of Self-Reported Guilt in Consumption Contexts." *Marketing Letters* 14 (October), 159–71.

Dahl, Darren W., Heather Honea, and Rajesh V. Manchanda (2005), "Three Rs of Interpersonal Consumer Guilt: Relationship, Reciprocity, Reparation." *Journal of Consumer Psychology* 15 (4), 307–15.

Dahlstrom, Robert, and Arne Nygaard (1995), "An Exploratory Investigation of Interpersonal Trust in New and Mature Market Economies." *Journal of Retailing* 71 (4), 339–61.

Dawson, Scott (1998), "Four Motivations for Charitable Giving: Implications for Marketing Strategy to Attract Monetary Donations for Medical Research." *Journal of Health Care Marketing* 8 (June), 31–7.

Day, George S. (1994), "The Capabilities of Market-Driven Organizations." *Journal of Marketing* 58 (October), 37–52.

Day, George S. (2000), "Managing Market Relationships." *Journal of the Academy of Marketing Science* 28 (1), 24–30.

Day, George S., and Robin Wensley (1988), "Assessing Advantage: A Framework for Diagnosing Competitive Superiority." *Journal of Marketing* 52 (April), 1–20.

De Wulf, Kristof, Gaby Odekerken-Schröder, and Dawn Iacobucci (2001), "Investments in Consumer Relationships: A Cross-Country and Cross-Industry Exploration." *Journal of Marketing* 65 (October), 33–50.

Dholakia, Ruby Roy, and Brian Sternthal (1977), "Highly Credible Sources: Persuasive Facilitators or Persuasive Liabilities?" *Journal of Consumer Research* 3 (March), 223–32.

Dick, Alan S., and Kunal Basu (1994), "Customer Loyalty: Toward an Integrated Conceptual Framework." *Journal of the Academy of Marketing Science* 22 (2), 99–113.

Diekmann, Andreas (2004), "The Power of Reciprocity: Fairness, Reciprocity, and Stakes in Variants of the Dictator." *Journal of Conflict Resolution* 48 (2004/08), 487–505.

Donaldson, Lee (2001), *The Contingency Theory of Organizations*. Thousand Oaks, Calif.: Sage Publications, Inc.

Doney, Patricia M., and Joseph P. Cannon (1997), "An Examination of the Nature of Trust in Buyer-Seller Relationships." *Journal of Marketing* 61 (April), 35–51.

Dowling, Grahame R., and Mark Uncles (1997), "Do Customer Loyalty Programs Really Work?" *Sloan Management Review* 38 (Summer), 71–82.

Drazin, Robert, and Andrew H. Van de Ven (1985), "Alternative Forms of Fit in Contingency Theory." *Administrative Science Quarterly* 30 (December), 514–39.

Dunn, Jennifer R., and Maurice E. Schweitzer (2005), "Feeling and Believing: The Influence of Emotion on Trust." *Journal of Personality & Social Psychology* 88 (5), 736–48.

Dwyer, Robert F., and Sejo Oh (1987), "Output Sector Munificence Effects on the Internal Political Economy of Marketing Channels." *Journal of Marketing Research* 24 (November), 347–58.

Dwyer, Robert F., Paul H. Schurr, and Sejo Oh (1987), "Developing Buyer-Seller Relationships." *Journal of Marketing* 51 (April), 11–27.

Dyer, Jeffrey H., and Harbir Singh (1998), "The Relational View: Cooperative Strategy and Sources of Interorganizational Competitive Advantage." *Academy of Management Review* 23 (4), 660–79.

Egan, John (2004), *Relationship Marketing: Exploring Relational Strategies in Marketing*, 2nd ed. London, U.K.: Financial Times/Prentice Hall.

El-Ansary, Adel I. (1975), "Determinants of Power-Dependence in Distribution Channel." *Journal of Retailing* 51 (Summer), 59–94.

Elahee, Mohammad N., Susan Kirby, and Ercan Nasif (2002), "National Culture, Trust, and Perceptions about Ethical Behavior in Intra- and Cross-Cultural Negotiations: An Analysis of NAFTA Countries." *Thunderbird International Business Review* 44 (November), 799–818.

Elangovan, A. R., and D. L. Shapiro (1998), "Betrayal of Trust in Organizations." *Academy of Management Review* 23 (3), 547–66.

Emerson, Richard M. (1962), "Power-Dependence Relations." *American Sociological Review* 27 (February), 31–41.

Emmons, Robert A., and Michael E. McCullough (2004), *The Psychology of Gratitude*. New York, N.Y.: Oxford University Press.

Eyuboglu, Nermin, and Andreas Buja (2007), "Quasi-Darwinian Selection in Marketing Relationships." *Journal of Marketing* 71 (October), 48–62.

Fang, Eric, Robert W. Palmatier, Lisa K. Scheer, and Ning Li (2008), "Trust at Different Organizational Levels." *Journal of Marketing* 72 (March), forthcoming.

Fiske, Susan T. (1980), "Attention and Weight in Person Perception: The Impact of Negative and Extreme Behavior." *Journal of Personality and Social Psychology* 38 (June), 889–906.

Frazier, Gary L. (1983), "On the Measurement of Interfirm Power in Channels of Distribution." *Journal of Marketing Research* 20 (May), 158–66.

Ganesan, Shankar (1994), "Determinants of Long-Term Orientation in Buyer-Seller Relationships." *Journal of Marketing* 58 (April), 1–19.

Garbarino, Ellen, and Mark S. Johnson (1999), "The Different Roles of Satisfaction, Trust, and Commitment in Customer Relationships." *Journal of Marketing* 63 (April), 70–87.

Gaski, John F. (1984), "The Theory of Power and Conflict in Channels of Distribution." *Journal of Marketing* 48 (Summer), 9–29.

Gassenheimer, Jule B., J. Charlene Davis, and Robert Dahlstrom (1998), "Is Dependent What We Want To Be? Effects of Incongruency." *Journal of Retailing* 74 (2), 247–71.

Goei, Ryan, and Franklin J. Boster (2005), "The Roles of Obligation and Gratitude in Explaining the Effect of Favors on Compliance." *Communication Monographs* 72 (September), 284–300.

Gouldner, Alvin W. (1960), "The Norm of Reciprocity: A Preliminary Statement." *American Sociology Review* 25 (April), 161–78.

Granovetter, Mark (1983), "The Strength of Weak Ties: A Network Theory Revisited." *Sociological Theory* 1 (1), 201–33.

Grayson, Kent, and Tim Ambler (1999), "The Dark Side of Long-Term Relationships in Marketing Services." *Journal of Marketing Research* 36 (February), 132–41.

Grönroos, Christian (1994), "From Marketing Mix to Relationship Marketing: Towards a Paradigm Shift in Marketing." *Management Decision* 32 (2), 4–20.

Grönroos, Christian (1997), "Value-Driven Relational Marketing: From Products to Resources and Competencies." *Journal of Marketing Management* 13 (4), 407–19.

Gundlach, Gregory T., Ravi S. Achrol, and John T. Mentzer (1995), "The Structure of Commitment in Exchange." *Journal of Marketing* 59 (January), 78–92.

Gwinner, Kevin P., Dwayne D. Gremler, and Mary Jo Bitner (1998), "Relational Benefits in Services Industries: The Customer's Perspective." *Journal of the Academy of Marketing Science* 26 (2), 101–14.

Håkansson, Håkan, and Ivan J. Snehota (2000), "The IMP Perspective: Assets and Liabilities of Business Relationships." In *The Handbook of Relationship Marketing*, eds. Jagdish N. Sheth and Atul Parvatiyar, 69-94. Thousands Oaks, Calif.: Sage Publications, Inc.

Hamilton, David L., and Steven J. Sherman (1996), "Perceiving Persons and Groups." *Psychological Review* 103 (April), 336–55.

Harker, Michael John (1999), "Relationship Marketing Defined? An Examination of Current Relationship Marketing Definitions." *Marketing Intelligence & Planning* 17 (1), 13–20.

Heide, Jan B. (1994), "Interorganizational Governance in Marketing Channels." *Journal of Marketing* 58 (January), 71–85.

Heide, Jan B., and George John (1988), "The Role of Dependence Balancing in Safeguarding Transaction-Specific Assets in Conventional Channels."

Journal of Marketing 52 (January), 20–35.

Heide, Jan B., and George John (1990), "Alliances in Industrial Purchasing: The Determinants of Joint Action in Buyer-Supplier Relationships." *Journal of Marketing Research* 27 (February), 24–36.

Heide, Jan B., and George John (1992), "Do Norms Matter in Marketing Relationships?" *Journal of Marketing* 56 (April), 32–44.

Hennig-Thurau, Thorsten, Kevin P. Gwinner, and Dwayne D. Gremler (2002), "Understanding Relationship Marketing Outcomes: An Integration of Relational Benefits and Relationship Quality." *Journal of Service Research* 4 (February), 230–47.

Hess, Ron L., Shankar Ganesan, and Noreen M. Klein (2003), "Service Failure and Recovery: The Impact of Relationship Factors on Customer Satisfaction." *Journal of the Academy of Marketing Science* 31 (2), 127–45.

Hewett, Kelly, and William O. Bearden (2001), "Dependence, Trust, and Relational Behavior on the Part of Foreign Subsidiary Marketing Operations: Implications for Managing Global Marketing Operations." *Journal of Marketing* 65 (October), 51–66.

Hewett, Kelly, Bruce R. Money, and Subhash Sharma (2002), "An Exploration of the Moderating Role of Buyer Corporate Culture in Industrial Buyer-Seller Relationships." *Journal of the Academy of Marketing Science* 30 (3), 229–39.

Hewett, Kelly, Bruce R. Money, and Subhash Sharma (2006), "National Culture and Industrial Buyer-Seller Relationships in the United States and Latin America." *Journal of the Academy of Marketing Science* 34 (3), 386–402.

Hibbard, Jonathan D., Frederic F. Brunel, Rajiv P. Dant, and Dawn Iacobucci (2001), "Does Relationship Marketing Age Well?" *Business Strategy Review* 12 (4), 29–35.

Hibbard, Jonathan D., Nirmalya Kumar, and Louis W. Stern (2001), "Examining the Impact of Destructive Acts in Marketing Channels Relationships." *Journal of Marketing Research* 38 (February), 25–61.

Hilton, John L., and William von Hippel (1990), "The Role of Consistency in Judgment of Stereotype-Relevant Behaviors." *Personality and Social Psychology Bulletin* 16 (1), 430–48.

Hofstede, Geert (1997), *Cultures and Organizations: Software of the Mind.* New York, N.Y.: McGraw-Hill.

Homburg, Christian, and Christian Pflesser (2000), "A Multiple-Layer Model of Market-Oriented Organizational Culture: Measurement Issues and Performance Outcomes." *Journal of Marketing Research* 37 (November), 449–62.

Houston, Mark B., Michael Hutt, Christine Moorman, Peter H. Reingen, Aric Rindfleisch, Vanitha Swaminathan, and Beth Walker (2004), "A Network Perspective on Marketing Strategy Research." In *Assessing Marketing Strategy Performance*, eds. Christine Moorman and Donald R. Lehman, 247–68. Cambridge, Mass.: Marketing Science Institute.

Hunt, Shelby D. (1983), "General Theories and the Fundamental Explanada of Marketing." *Journal of Marketing* 47 (Fall), 9–17.

Iacobucci, Dawn, and Amy Ostrom (1996), "Commercial and Interpersonal Relationships; Using the Structure of Interpersonal Relationships to Understand Individual-to-Individual, Individual-to-Firm, and Firm-to-Firm Relationships in Commerce." *International Journal of Research in Marketing* 13 (1), 53–72.

Jacobs, Robert C., and Donald T. Campbell (1961), "The Perpetuation of an Arbitrary Tradition Through Several Generations of a Laboratory Microculture." *Journal of Abnormal and Social Psychology* 62 (3), 649–58.

Jacoby, Jacob, and Robert W. Chestnut (1978), *Brand Loyalty*. New York, N.Y.: John Wiley & Sons.

Jap, Sandy D. (1999), "Pie-Expansion Efforts: Collaboration Processes in Buyer-Supplier Relationships." *Journal of Marketing Research* 36 (November), 461–75.

Jap, Sandy D., and Erin Anderson (2007), "Testing a Life-Cycle Theory of Cooperative Interorganizational Relationships: Movement across Stages and Performance." *Management Science* 53 (February), 260–75.

Jap, Sandy D., and Shankar Ganesan (2000), "Control Mechanisms and the Relationship Life Cycle: Implications for Safeguarding Specific Investments and Developing Commitment." *Journal of Marketing Research* 37 (May), 227–45.

Jaworski, Bernard J., and Ajay K. Kohli (1993), "Market Orientation: Antecedents and Consequences." *Journal of Marketing* 57 (July), 53–70.

John, George (1984), "An Empirical Investigation of Some Antecedents of Opportunism in a Marketing Channel." *Journal of Marketing Research* 21 (August), 278–89.

Johnson, D. W., and S. Johnson (1972), "The Effects of Attitude Similarity, Expectation of Goal Facilitation, and Actual Goal Facilitation on Interpersonal Attraction." *Journal of Experimental Social Psychology* 8 (3), 197–206.

Johnson, Jean L. (1999), "Strategic Integration in Industrial Distribution Channels: Managing the Interfirm Relationship as a Strategic Asset." *Journal of the Academy of Marketing Science* 27 (1), 4–18.

Johnson, Jean L., and Ravipreet S. Sohi (2001), "The Influence of Firm

Predispositions on Interfirm Relationship Formation in Business Markets." *International Journal of Research in Marketing* 18 (4), 299–318.

Johnson, Michael D., and Fred Selnes (2004), "Customer Portfolio Management: Toward a Dynamic Theory of Exchange Relationships." *Journal of Marketing* 68 (April), 1–17.

Joshi, Ashwin W., and Rodney L. Stump (1999), "The Contingent Effect of Specific Asset Investments on Joint Action in Manufacturer-Supplier Relationships: An Empirical Test of the Moderating Role of Reciprocal Assets Investments, Uncertainty, and Trust." *Journal of the Academy of Marketing Science* 27 (3), 291–305.

Kallgren, Carl A., Raymond R. Reno, and Robert B. Cialdini (2000), "A Focus Theory of Normative Conduct: When Norms Do and Do Not Affect Behavior." *Personality and Social Psychology Bulletin* 26 (August), 1002–12.

Kalwani, Manohar U., and Narakesari Narayandas (1995), "Long-Term Manufacturer-Supplier Relationships: Do They Pay Off for Supplier Firms?" *Journal of Marketing* 59 (January), 1–16.

Katrichis, Jerome M. (1998), "Exploring Departmental Level Interaction Patterns in Organizational Purchasing Decisions." *Industrial Marketing Management* 27 (March), 135–46.

Kaufmann, Patrick J., and Rajiv P. Dant (1992), "The Dimensions of Commercial Exchange." *Marketing Letters* 3 (April), 171–85.

Keller, Kevin Lane (1993), "Conceptualizing, Measuring, and Managing Customer-Based Brand Equity." *Journal of Marketing* 57 (January), 1–22.

Kumar, Nirmalya, Jonathan D. Hibbard, and Leonard D. Stern (1994), "The Nature and Consequences of Marketing Channel Intermediary Commitment." Cambridge, Mass.: Marketing Science Institute, Report No. 94-115.

Kumar, Nirmalya, Lisa K. Scheer, and Jan-Benedict E. M. Steenkamp (1995a), "The Effects of Perceived Interdependence on Dealer Attitudes." *Journal of Marketing Research* 32 (August), 348–56.

Kumar, Nirmalya, Lisa K. Scheer, and Jan-Benedict E. M. Steenkamp (1995b), "The Effects of Supplier Fairness on Vulnerable Resellers." *Journal of Marketing Research* 32 (February), 54–65.

Lagace, Rosemary R., Robert Dahlstrom, and Jule B. Gassenheimer (1991), "The Relevance of Ethical Salesperson Behavior on Relationship Quality: The Pharmaceutical Industry." *Journal of Personal Selling and Sales Management* 11 (Fall), 39–47.

Lewicki, Roy J., and Barbara B. Bunker, eds. (1996), *Developing and Maintaining Trust in Working Relationships*. Thousand Oaks, Calif.: Sage Publications, Inc.

Lewicki, Roy J., Daniel J. McAllister, and Robert J. Bies (1998), "Trust and Distrust: New Relationships and Realities." *Academy of Management Review* 23 (3), 438–58.

Lewicki, Roy J., Edward C. Tomlinson, and Nicole Gillespie (2006), "Models of Interpersonal Trust Development: Theoretical Approaches, Empirical Evidence, and Future Directions." *Journal of Management* 32 (December), 991–1022.

Li, Peter Ping (2007), "Social Tie, Social Capital, and Social Behavior: Toward an Integrative Model of Informal Exchange." *Asia Pacific Journal of Management* 24 (2), 227–46.

Lickel, Brian, David L. Hamilton, Amy Lewis, Steven J. Sherman, Grazyna Wieczorkowska, and A. Neville Uhles (2000), "Varieties of Group and the Perception of Group Entitativity." *Journal of Personality and Social Psychology* 78 (February), 223–46.

Luna-Reyes, Luis F., Anthony M. Cresswell, and George P. Richardson (2004), "Knowledge and the Development of Interpersonal Trust: A Dynamic Model." *Proceedings of Hawaii International Conference on System Sciences* 37 (January), 1–12.

Macaulay, Stewart (1963), "Non-Contractual Relations in Business." *American Sociological Review* 28 (1), 55–67.

Macintosh, Gerrard, and Lawrence S. Lockshin (1997), "Retail Relationships and Store Loyalty: A Multi-level Perspective." *International Journal of Research in Marketing* 14 (5), 487–97.

MacKenzie, Herbert F., and Kenneth G. Hardy (1996), "Manage Your Offering or Managing Your Relationship?" *Journal of Business & Industrial Marketing* 11 (6), 20–37.

Macneil, Ian (1980), *The New Social Contract: An Inquiry into Modern Contractual Relations*. New Haven, Conn.: Yale University Press.

Menon, Tanya, Michael W. Morris, Chi-yue Chiu, and Ying-yi Hong (1999), "Culture and the Construal of Agency: Attribution to Individual Versus Group Dispositions." *Journal of Personality and Social Psychology* 76 (May), 701–17.

Mithas, Sunil, M. S. Krishnan, and Claes Fornell (2005), "Why Do Customer Relationship Management Applications Affect Customer Satisfaction?" *Journal of Marketing* 69 (October), 201–9.

Mittal, Banwari (1995), "Comparative Analysis of Four Scales of Consumer Involvement." *Psychology & Marketing* 12 (7), 663–82.

Mittal, Vikas, Jerome M. Katrichas, and Pankaj Kumar (2001), "Attribute Performance and Customer Satisfaction over Time: Evidence from Two Field Studies." *Journal of Services Marketing* 15 (4/5), 343–57.

Mohr, Jakki J., Robert J. Fisher, and John R. Nevin (1996), "Collaborative Communication in Interfirm Relationships: Moderating Effects of Integration and Control." *Journal of Marketing* 60 (July), 103–15.

Mohr, Jakki J., and John R. Nevin (1990), "Communication Strategies in Marketing Channels: A Theoretical Perspective." *Journal of Marketing* 54 (October), 36–51.

Mohr, Jakki J., and Robert Spekman (1994), "Characteristics of Partnership Success: Partnership Attributes, Communication Behavior, and Conflict Resolution Techniques." *Strategic Management Journal* 15 (2), 135–52.

Mohrman, Susan A., Ramkrishnan V. Tenkasi, and Allan M. Mohrman (2003), "The Role of Networks in Fundamental Organizational Change." *Journal of Applied Behavioral Science* 39 (September), 301–23.

Moorman, Christine, Gerald Zaltman, and Rohit Deshpandé (1992), "Relationships Between Providers and Users of Market Research: The Dynamics of Trust within and Between Organizations." *Journal of Marketing Research* 29 (August), 314–29.

Morales, Andrea C. (2005), "Giving Firms an 'E' for Effort: Consumer Responses to High-Effort Firms." *Journal of Consumer Research* 31 (March), 806–12.

Morgan, Robert M. (2000), "Relationship Marketing and Marketing Strategy: The Evolution of Relationship Marketing Strategy Within the Organization." In *Handbook of Relationship Marketing*, eds. Jagdish N. Sheth and Atul Parvatiyar, 481–504. Thousand Oaks, Calif.: Sage Publications, Inc.

Morgan, Robert M., and Shelby D. Hunt (1994), "The Commitment-Trust Theory of Relationship Marketing." *Journal of Marketing* 58 (July), 20–38.

Ndubisi, Nelson O. (2004), "Understanding the Salience of Cultural Dimensions on Relationship Marketing, Its Underpinnings and Aftermaths." *Cross Cultural Management* 11 (3), 70–89.

Nicholson, Carolyn Y., Larry D. Compeau, and Rajesh Sethi (2001), "The Role of Interpersonal Liking in Building Trust in Long-Term Channel Relationships." *Journal of the Academy of Marketing Science* 29 (1), 3–15.

Noordewier, Thomas, George John, and John R. Nevin (1990), "Performance Outcomes of Purchasing Arrangements in Industrial Buyer-Vender Relationships." *Journal of Marketing* 54 (October), 80–93.

O'Laughlin, Matthew J., and Bertram F. Malle (2002), "How People Explain Actions Performed by Groups and Individuals." *Journal of Personality and Social Psychology* 82 (January), 33–48.

Oliver, Richard L. (1999), "Whence Consumer Loyalty?" *Journal of Marketing* 63 (Special Issue), 33–44.

Oliver, Richard L., and Erin Anderson (1994), "An Empirical Test of the Consequences of Behavior and Outcome-Based Sales Control Systems." *Journal of Marketing* 58 (October), 53–67.

O'Reilly, Charles A., and Jennifer A. Chatman (1996), "Culture as Social Control: Corporations, Cults and Commitment." In *Research in Organizational Behavior*, vol. 18, eds. B. Staw and L. Cummings, 157–200. Greenwich, Conn.: JAI Press.

Ostrom, Elinor, and James Walker, eds. (2003), *Trust and Reciprocity: Interdisciplinary Lessons from Experimental Research*. New York, N.Y.: Russell Sage Foundation.

Palmatier, Robert W. (2007), "What Drives Customer Relationship Value in Business-to-Business Exchanges?" Cambridge, Mass.: Marketing Science Institute, Report No. 07-118.

Palmatier, Robert W. (2008), "Interfirm Relational Drivers of Customer Value." *Journal of Marketing* (July), forthcoming.

Palmatier, Robert W., Rajiv P. Dant, and Dhruv Grewal (2007), "A Comparative Longitudinal Analysis of Theoretical Perspectives of Interorganizational Relationship Performance." *Journal of Marketing* 71 (October), 172–94.

Palmatier, Robert W., Rajiv P. Dant, Dhruv Grewal, and Kenneth R. Evans (2006), "Factors Influencing the Effectiveness of Relationship Marketing: A Meta-Analysis." *Journal of Marketing* 70 (October), 136–53.

Palmatier, Robert W., Rajiv P. Dant, Dhruv Grewal, and Mark B. Houston (2007a), "Relationship Marketing Dynamics." Seattle, Wash.: University of Washington Working Paper 1 (September), 1–37.

Palmatier, Robert W., Srinath Gopalakrishna, and Mark B. Houston (2006), "Returns on Business-to-Business Relationship Marketing Investments: Strategies for Leveraging Profits." *Marketing Science* 25 (September-October), 477–93.

Palmatier, Robert W., Cheryl Burke Jarvis, Jennifer Beckhoff, and Frank R. Kardes (2007b), "Micro-Theory of Relationship Marketing," Seattle, Wash.: University of Washington Working Paper 2 (December), 1–33.

Palmatier, Robert W., Lisa Scheer, Kenneth R. Evan, and Todd Arnold (2008), "Achieving Relationship Marketing Effectiveness in Business-to-Business Exchanges." *Journal of the Academy of Marketing Science*, forthcoming.

Palmatier, Robert W., Lisa K. Scheer, Mark B. Houston, Kenneth R. Evans, and Srinath Gopalakrishna (2007c), "Use of Relationship Marketing Programs in Building Customer-Salesperson and Customer-Firm Relationships: Differential Influences on Financial Outcomes." *International Journal of Research in Marketing* 24 (September), 210–23.

Palmatier, Robert W., Lisa K. Scheer, and J. B. Steenkamp (2007), "Customer Loyalty to Whom? Managing the Benefits and Risks of Salesperson-Owned Loyalty." *Journal of Marketing Research* 44 (May), 185–99.

Payne, Adrian, and Pennie Frow (2005), "A Strategic Framework for Customer Relationship Management." *Journal of Marketing* 69 (October), 167–76.

Pfeffer, Jeffrey, and Gerald R. Salancik (1978), *The External Control of Organizations: A Resource Dependence Approach.* New York, N.Y.: Harper and Row Publishers.

Rackham, Neil (1996), *The SPIN Selling Fieldbook.* New York, N.Y.: McGraw-Hill Professional Publishing.

Rangan, Subramanian (2000), "The Problem of Search and Deliberation in Economic Actions: When Social Networks Really Matter." *Academy of Management Review* 25 (4), 813–28.

Reichheld, Frederick F. (2001), "Lead for Loyalty." *Harvard Business Review* 79 (7), 76–84.

Reichheld, Fredrick F. (2003), "The One Number You Need." *Harvard Business Review* 81 (December), 46-54.

Reichheld, Fredrick F., and Thomas Teal (1996), *The Loyalty Effect.* Boston, Mass.: Harvard Business School Press.

Reinartz, Werner J., Manfred Krafft, and Wayne D. Hoyer (2004), "The Customer Relationship Management Process: Its Measurement and Impact on Performance." *Journal of Marketing Research* 41 (August), 293–305.

Reinartz, Werner J., and V. Kumar (2000), "On the Profitability of Long-Life Customers in a Noncontractual Setting: An Empirical Investigation and Implications for Marketing." *Journal of Marketing* 64 (October), 17–35.

Reynolds, Kristy E., and Sharon E. Beatty (1999), "Customer Benefits and Company Consequences of Customer-Salesperson Relationships in Retailing." *Journal of Retailing* 75 (1), 11–32.

Rindfleisch, Aric, and Jan B. Heide (1997), "Transaction Cost Analysis: Past, Present, and Future Applications." *Journal of Marketing* 61 (October), 30–54.

Rindfleisch, Aric, and Christine Moorman (2001), "The Acquisition and Utilization of Information in New Product Alliances: A Strength-of-Ties Perspective." *Journal of Marketing* 65 (April), 1–18.

Rindfleisch, Aric, and Christine Moorman (2003), "Interfirm Cooperation and Customer Orientation." *Journal of Marketing Research* 40 (11), 421–36.

Ring, Peter Smith, and Andrew H. Van de Ven (1994), "Developmental Processes of Cooperative Interorganizational Relationships." *Academy of Management Review* 19 (1), 90–118.

Rousseau, Denise M., Sim B. Sitkin, Ronald S. Burt, and Colin Camerer (1998), "Not So Different After All: A Cross-Discipline View of Trust." *Academy of Management Review* 23 (3), 393–404.

Rowley, Timothy J. (1997), "Moving Beyond Dyadic Ties: A Network Theory of Stakeholder Influences." *Academy of Management Review* 22 (4), 887–910.

Rust, Roland T., Katherine N. Lemon, and Valarie A. Zeithaml (2004), "Return on Marketing: Using Customer Equity to Focus Marketing Strategy." *Journal of Marketing* 68 (January), 109–27.

Rust, Roland T., Valarie A. Zeithaml, and Katherine N. Lemon (2000), *Driving Customer Equity: How Customer Lifetime Value Is Reshaping Corporate Strategy*. New York, N.Y.: Free Press.

Samiee, Saeed, and Peter G. P. Walters (2003), "Relationship Marketing in an International Context: A Literature Review." *International Business Review* 12 (2), 193–214.

Schutz, Will (1992), "Beyond FIRO-B—Three New Theory-Derived Measures—Elements B: Behavior, Elements F: Feelings, Elements S: Self." *Psychological Reports* 70, 915–37.

Schwartz, Barry (1967), "The Social Psychology of the Gift." *The American Journal of Sociology* 73 (July), 1–11.

Sheth, Jagdish N., and Atul Parvatiyar (1995), "The Evolution of Relationship Marketing." *International Business Review* 4 (4), 397–418.

Sheth, Jagdish N., and Atul Parvatiyar (2000), *Handbook of Relationship Marketing*. Thousands Oaks, Calif.: Sage Publications, Inc.

Shiv, Baba, Julie A. Edell, and John W. Payne (1997), "Factors Affecting the Impact of Negatively and Positively Framed Ad Messages." *Journal of Consumer Research* 24 (December), 285–94.

Siguaw, Judy A., Penny M. Simpson, and Thomas L. Baker (1998), "Effects of Supplier Market Orientation on Distributor Market Orientation and the Channel Relationship: The Distributor Perspective." *Journal of Marketing* 62 (July), 99–111.

Sirdeshmukh, Deepak, Jagdip Singh, and Barry Sabol (2002), "Consumer Trust, Value, and Loyalty in Relational Exchanges." *Journal of Marketing* 66 (January), 15–37.

Sivadas, Eugene, and Robert F. Dwyer (2000), "An Examination of Organizational Factors Influencing New Product Success in Internal and Alliance-Based Processes." *Journal of Marketing* 64 (January), 31–49.

Smith, J. Brock, and Donald W. Barclay (1997), "The Effects of Organizational Differences and Trust on the Effectiveness of Selling Partner Relationships." *Journal of Marketing* 61 (January), 3–21.

Spekman, Robert E. (1988), "Strategic Supplier Selection: Understanding Long-Term Relationships." *Business Horizons* 31 (July/August), 75–81.

Srivastava, Rajendra K., Tasadduq A. Shervani, and Liam Fahey (1998), "Market-Based Assets and Shareholder Value: A Framework for Analysis." *Journal of Marketing* 62 (January), 2–18.

Stern, Louis W., and Torger Reve (1980), "Distribution Channels as Political Economies: A Framework for Comparative Analysis." *Journal of Marketing* 44 (Summer), 52–64.

Stevenson, William B., and Danna Greenberg (2000), "Agency and Social Networks: Strategies of Action in Social Structure of Position, Opposition, and Opportunity." *Administrative Science Quarterly* 45 (December), 651–78.

Tax, Stephen S., and Stephen W. Brown (1998), "Recovering and Learning from Service Failure." *Sloan Management Review* 40 (1), 75–88.

Tesser, Abraham, Robert Gatewood, and Michael Driver (1968), "Some Determinants of Gratitude." *Journal of Personality and Social Psychology* 9 (3), 233–6.

Thibaut, John W., and Harold H. Kelley (1959), *The Social Psychology of Groups*. New York, N.Y.: John Wiley & Sons.

Trachtenberg, Jeffrey (2007), "Borders Slashes Buyer Rewards, Cuts Discounts." *Wall Street Journal*, D1.

Trivers, Robert (1971), "The Evolution of Reciprocal Altruism." *Quarterly Review of Biology* 46 (March), 35–57.

Trivers, Robert (1985), *Social Evolution*. Menlo Park, Calif.: The Benjamin/ Cummins Publishing Company, Inc.

Tsai, Wenpin (2001), "Knowledge Transfer in Interorganizational Networks: Effects of Network Position and Absorptive Capacity on Business Unit Innovation and Performance." *Academy of Management Journal* 44 (October), 996–1001.

Tsang, Jo-Ann (2006), "The Effects of Helper Intention on Gratitude and Indebtedness." *Motivation & Emotion* 30 (September), 198–204.

Tushman, Michael L., and David A. Nadler (1978), "Information Processing as an Integrating Concept in Organizational Design." *Academy of Management Review* 3 (3), 613–24.

Van den Bulte, Christophe, and Stefan Wuyts (2007), *Social Networks and Marketing*. Cambridge, Mass.: Marketing Science Institute.

Vargo, Stephen L., and Robert F. Lusch (2004), "Evolving to a New Dominant Logic for Marketing." *Journal of Marketing* 68 (January), 1–17.

Venkatesan, Rajkumar, and V. Kumar (2004), "A Customer Lifetime Value

Framework for Customer Selection and Resource Allocation Strategy." *Journal of Marketing* 68 (October), 106–25.

Verhoef, Peter C. (2003), "Understanding the Effect of Customer Relationship Management Efforts on Customer Retention and Customer Share Development." *Journal of Marketing* 67 (October), 30–45.

Verhoef, Peter C., Philip Hans Franses, and Janny C. Hoekstra (2002), "The Effect of Relational Constructs on Customer Referrals and Number of Services Purchased from a Multiservice Provider: Does Age of Relationship Matter?" *Journal of the Academy of Marketing Science* 30 (3), 202–16.

Walker, Gordon, Bruce Kogut, and Weijan Shan (1997), "Social Capital, Structural Holes and the Formation of Industry Networks." *Organization Science* 8 (March-April), 109–25.

Wasserman, Stanley, and Katherine Faust (1994), *Social Network Analysis.* Cambridge, U.K.: Cambridge University Press.

Wathne, Kenneth H., and Jan B. Heide (2000), "Opportunism in Interfirm Relationships: Forms, Outcomes, and Solutions." *Journal of Marketing* 64 (October), 36–51.

Watkins, Philip C., Kathrane Woodward, Tamara Stone, and Russell L. Kolts (2003), "Gratitude and Happiness: Development of a Measure of Gratitude, and Relationships with Subjective Well-Being." *Social Behavior & Personality: An International Journal* 31, 431–51.

Weiner, Bernard (1985), "An Attributional Theory of Achievement Motivation and Emotion." *Psychological Review* 92 (4), 548–73.

Weiner, Bernard (1986), *An Attributional Theory of Motivation and Emotion.* New York, N.Y.: Springer-Verlag.

Weinzimmer, Laurence G., Edward U. Bond, Mark B. Houston, and Paul C. Nystrom (2003), "Relating Marketing Expertise on the Top Management Team and Strategic Market Aggressiveness to Financial Performance and Shareholder Value." *Journal of Strategic Marketing* 11 (June), 133–59.

Weiss, Allan M., and Erin Anderson (1992), "Converting from Independent to Employee Salesforce: The Role of Perceived Switching Costs." *Journal of Marketing Research* 29 (February), 101–15.

Weitz, Barton A., and Kevin D. Bradford (1999), "Personal Selling and Sales Management: A Relationship Marketing Perspective." *Journal of the Academy of Marketing Science* 27 (2), 241–54.

Weitz, Barton A., Harish Sujan, and Mita Sujan (1986), "Knowledge, Motivation, and Adaptive Behavior: A Framework for Improving Selling Effectiveness." *Journal of Marketing* 50 (October), 174–91.

Wernerfelt, Birger (1984), "A Resource-Based View of the Firm." *Strategic Management Journal* 5 (2), 171–80.

Whatley, Mark A., J. Matthew Webster, Richard H. Smith, and Adele Rhodes (1999), "The Effect of a Favor on Public and Private Compliance: How Internalized Is the Norm of Reciprocity?" *Basic and Applied Social Psychology* 21 (September), 251–9.

Williamson, Oliver E. (1975), *Markets and Hierarchies: Analysis and Antitrust Implications.* New York, N.Y.: The Free Press.

Williamson, Oliver E. (1981), "The Economics of Organization: The Transaction Cost Approach." *American Journal of Sociology* 87 (November), 548–77.

Williamson, Oliver E. (1985), *The Economic Institute of Capitalism: Firms, Markets, Relational Contracting.* New York, N.Y.: The Free Press.

Wilson, David T. (1995), "An Integrated Model of Buyer-Seller Relationships." *Journal of the Academy of Marketing Science* 23 (4), 335–45.

Young, Louise (2006), "Trust: Looking Forward and Back." *Journal of Business & Industrial Marketing* 21 (7), 439–45.

Zeithaml, Valarie A., A. Parasuraman, and Leonard L. Berry (1985), "Problems and Strategies in Services Marketing." *Journal of Marketing* 49 (Spring), 33–46.

ABOUT THE AUTHOR

Robert W. Palmatier (palmatrw@u.washington.edu) is Evert McCabe Faculty Fellow and Assistant Professor at the University of Washington. Prior to academia, he held numerous positions in industry including President and Chief Operating Officer of C&K Components, and European General Manager and Sales and Marketing Manager at multiple divisions of Tyco-Raychem Corporation. He has also served as a Lieutenant on board nuclear submarines in the United States Navy.

Palmatier has served as the chair of the National Research Council, the National Academy of Sciences, and the Wright Centers of Innovation proposal selection committee, which awarded grants of $20 million for the development of a new Wright Center of Innovation. He was selected as a member of NASA's Computing, Information, and Communications Advisory Group to assess the current state of technology development within academia, governmental agencies, and industry for recommending future investments areas. He has worked as a marketing consultant with companies including Cincom, Emerson, Fifth Third Bank, Littelfuse, Microsoft, and Manufacturers' Representative Educational Research Foundation.

His research is focused on relationship marketing and business strategy with an emphasis on multi-channel customer relationships in business-to-business and retail markets. His research has appeared in the *Journal of Marketing*, *Journal of Marketing Research*, *Marketing Science*, *Journal of the Academy of Marketing Science*, and *International Journal of Research in Marketing*.

Palmatier holds bachelor's and master's degrees in electrical engineering from Georgia Institute of Technology, an M.B.A. from Georgia State University, and a Ph.D. from the University of Missouri.

ABOUT MSI

Founded in 1961, the Marketing Science Institute is a learning organization dedicated to bridging the gap between marketing science theory and business practice. MSI currently brings together executives from approximately 70 sponsoring corporations with leading researchers from over 100 universities worldwide.

As a nonprofit institution, MSI financially supports academic research for the development—and practical translation—of leading-edge marketing knowledge on topics of importance to business. Issues of key importance to business performance are identified by the Board of Trustees, which represents MSI corporations and the academic community. MSI supports studies by academics on these issues and disseminates the results through conferences and workshops, as well as through its publications series.

Related MSI Working Papers

02-123 "Superiority in Customer Relationship Management: Consequences for Competitive Advantage and Performance" by George S. Day and Christophe Van den Bulte

02-113 "Are Customer Information Systems Worth It? Results from B2B Services" by Debra Zahay and Abbie Griffin

01-116 "Consumer Trust, Value, and Loyalty in Relational Exchanges" by Deepak Sirdeshmukh, Jagdip Singh, and Barry Sabol

01-108 "Driving Customer Equity: Linking Customer Lifetime Value to Strategic Marketing Decisions" by Roland T. Rust, Katherine N. Lemon, and Valarie A. Zeithaml

00-120 "Getting Returns from Service Quality: Is the Conventional Wisdom Wrong?" by Roland T. Rust, Christine Moorman, and Peter R. Dickson

00-118 "Capabilities for Forging Customer Relationships" by George S. Day

99-103 "Relationship Learning with Key Customers" by Fred Selnes and James Sallis